TURNER (**JIDES**

The Tauris British ... in 2003, contributed to the re... ʒ in-depth key British films from the past hundred years. ... project forward I.B.Tauris has now entered an exciting and innovative partnership with TCM (Turner Classic Movies), the premier movie channel dedicated to keeping the classic movies alive for fans old and new. With a striking new design and new identity, the series will continue to provide what the *Guardian* has called 'a valuable resource of critical work on the UK's neglected film history'. Each film guide will establish the historical and cinematic context of the film, provide a detailed critical reading and assess the reception and after-life of the production. The series will continue to draw on all genres and all eras, building over time into a wide-ranging library of informed, in-depth books on the films that will comprehensively refute the ill-informed judgement of French director François Truffaut that there was a certain incompatibility between the terms British and cinema. It will demonstrate the variety, creativity, humanity, poetry and mythic power of the best of British cinema in volumes designed to be accessible to film enthusiasts, scholars and students alike.

TCM is the definitive classic movie channel available on cable, satellite and digital terrestrial TV <www.tcmonline.co.uk>.

JEFFREY RICHARDS
General Editor

British Film Guides published and forthcoming:

Whiskey Galore! and The Maggie Colin McArthur
The Charge of the Light Brigade Mark Connelly
Get Carter Steve Chibnall
Dracula Peter Hutchings
The Private Life of Henry VIII Greg Walker
My Beautiful Laundrette Christine Geraghty
Brighton Rock Steve Chibnall
A Hard Day's Night Stephen Glynn
If Paul Sutton
Black Narcissus Sarah Street
The Red Shoes Mark Connelly
Saturday Night and Sunday Morning Anthony Aldgate
A Clockwork Orange I.Q. Hunter
Four Weddings and a Funeral Andrew Spicer

TURNER CLASSIC MOVIE BRITISH FILM GUIDE

A Hard Day's Night
STEPHEN GLYNN

I.B. TAURIS
LONDON · NEW YORK

Published in 2005 by I.B.Tauris & Co Ltd
6 Salem Road, London W2 4BU
175 Fifth Avenue, New York NY 10010
www.ibtauris.com

In the United States of America and Canada distributed by Palgrave Macmillan
a division of St Martin's Press, 175 Fifth Avenue, New York NY 10010

Copyright © Stephen Glynn, 2005

The TCM logo and trademark and all related elements are trademarks of and
© Turner Entertainment Networks International Limited. A Time Warner
Company. All Rights Reserved. © and ™ 2005 Turner Entertainment Networks
International Limited.

The right of Stephen Glynn to be identified as the author of this work has
been asserted by him in accordance with the Copyright, Designs and Patents
Act, 1988.

All rights reserved. Except for brief quotations in a review, this book, or any
part thereof, may not be reproduced in any form without permission in writing
from the publisher.

ISBN 1 85043 587 1
EAN 978 1 85043 587 7

A full CIP record for this book is available from the British Library
A full CIP record for this book is available from the Library of Congress

Library of Congress catalog card: available

Set in Monotype Fournier and Univers Black by Ewan Smith, London
Printed and bound in Great Britain by TJ International Ltd, Padstow, Cornwall

Contents

    List of Illustrations / vi

    Credits   1
1   Context   3
2   Analysis   33
3   Reception and Afterlife   82

    Notes   95
    Sources   100

Illustrations

1. 'From Me to You'. A film awash with images of the Beatles, 'black-and-white people'.   19
2. 'Powdered Gee-gaws'. Paul as actor: a bit of Shakespeare that did not hit the cutting-room floor.   20
3. 'Real Love'. Enjoyment in entrapment (and a glaring continuity error in John's attire).   26
4. 'If I Fell'. Immediate claustrophobia.   40
5. 'Charley Peace'. Ringo as Charley (Chaplin).   52
6. 'Day Tripper'. John feeds his Coke habit.   54
7. 'Two-faced Trouble-maker'. John as Janus.   56
8. 'Feeling You Holding Me Tight'. Patti meets George, and Freud.   59
9. 'Pop Art'. Richard + George = Andy + Jackie.   60
10. 'I Work All Day'. Music as Labour.   69
11. 'Free as a Bird'. The escape into non-performative illustration.   71
12. 'Tell Me What You See'. Music plus mediation.   73
13. 'She Loves You'. The climax, as boy meets girl.   77
14. 'You Know My Name'. The consummate professionals, professing instant and copious consumption.   80

Film Credits

Released by	United Artists
Production Company	Proscenium Films
Producer	Walter Shenson
Director	Richard Lester
Scriptwriter	Alun Owen
Associate Producer	Denis O'Dell
Director of Photography	Gilbert Taylor BSC
Musical Director	George Martin
Songs by	John Lennon and Paul McCartney
Art Director	Ray Simm
Editor	John Jympson
Assistant Director	John D. Merriman
Camera Operator	Derek V. Browne
Costume Designer	Julie Harris
Beatles' Wardrobe	Dougie Millings and Son
Make-up	John O'Gorman
Hairdressing	Betty Glasgow
Continuity	Rita Davison
Titles Design	Robert Freeman
Sound Recordists	H. L. Bird and Stephen Dalby
Sound Editor	Gordon Daniel
Assistant Editor	Pamela Tomling

Uncredited:

Executive Producer	David V. Picker
Assistant Editor	Roy Benson
Second Assistant Director	Barrie Melrose
Camera Operator	Paul Wilson
Sound Editor	Jim Roddan
Length	7,650 feet
Running Time	85 minutes
UK Première	6 July 1964
US Première	12 August 1964

CAST

John Lennon	John
Paul McCartney	Paul
George Harrison	George
Ringo Starr	Ringo
Wilfrid Brambell	Grandfather
Norman Rossington	Norm
John Junkin	Shake
Victor Spinetti	TV director
Anna Quayle	Millie
Deryck Guyler	Police Inspector
Richard Vernon	Man on train – Johnson
Eddie Malin	Hotel waiter
Robin Ray	TV floor manager
Lionel Blair	TV choreographer
Alison Seebohm	Secretary
David Jaxon	Young boy – Charley
Uncredited:	
Isla Blair	Shakespearean actress (scenes deleted)
Bridget Armstrong	Lead make-up woman
Roger Avon	Actor
Pru Berry	Rita – brunette schoolgirl on train
John Bluthal	Man stealing car
Patti Boyd	Jean – blonde schoolgirl on train
Phil Collins	Seated fan with necktie
Rosemarie Frankland	Brunette showgirl
Kenneth Haigh	Simon Marshall
Julian Holloway	Adrian, Simon's assistant
Terry Hooper	Croupier
Clare Kelly	Barmaid
David Langton	Actor
Jeremy Lloyd	Tall dancer at the disco
Derek Nimmo	Leslie Jackson, magician
Margaret Nolan	Girl at casino
Marianne Stone	Society reporter
Michael Trubshawe	Casino manager

ONE
Context

WHY DON'T WE DO THE SHOW RIGHT HERE!

In 1999 the British Film Institute asked a thousand people from all strands of the film and television industries throughout the United Kingdom – producers, directors, writers, actors, technicians, academics, exhibitors, distributors, executives and critics – to vote for the 'culturally British' feature films, released in cinemas during the twentieth century, that they felt had made a strong and lasting impression. The resultant 'BFI Top 100' makes for interesting reading. The expected canonical works are dominant: *The Third Man*, *Brief Encounter*, *Lawrence of Arabia*, *The Thirty-nine Steps*, *Great Expectations*, *Kind Hearts and Coronets* and *The Red Shoes*. These are well-loved British favourites and evidently merit their selection. But there are edgier, quirkier choices too. At number 88, flanked by Ken Russell's adaptation of D. H. Lawrence's *Women in Love* (1969) and Humphrey Jennings's London Blitz documentary *Fires were Started* (1943), is a 1964 pop musical, made in a matter of weeks and intended as an instantly disposable cash-in on a passing adolescent fad. Generations later, it is perceived as worthy of a place in the British cinematic pantheon. The enduring appeal of *A Hard Day's Night* lies predominantly in the ageless charm of its protagonists, four lads from Liverpool who changed for ever the style, the content and the significance of popular music around the world. But their debut film also effected a paradigm shift in the sub-genre of the pop musical, proving quickly, through its innovative power, to be both apogee and executioner.

The early history of pop music is inextricably linked to its cinematic illustration, while the life-span of the British pop musical is roughly concurrent with what Arthur Marwick has termed 'the long sixties'.[1] For Marwick, 'some time between the early fifties and the early seventies a "cultural revolution" took place in Britain' resulting in the creation of distinctive cultural artefacts including 'pop music (above all)'.[2] Jeffrey

Richards and Anthony Aldgate specify the starting point, writing that 'the years 1956–58 were to represent a cultural watershed, energizing society with a cultural revolt which was to lead in due course to political change' and which also 'saw the arrival of rock music from the United States' and 'the first steps towards the development of the distinctive youth culture that was to flow into the 1960s and took the form of protest against established canons of taste, decency and respectability'.[3]

Cinema is central to this cultural transference and transgression. In an age before dedicated pop music channels on radio and television, celluloid was the prime medium for the dissemination of new sounds and social styles. The last-minute use of Bill Haley's 'Rock Around the Clock' over the opening and closing credits of Richard Brooks's analysis of social deprivation and juvenile delinquency, *The Blackboard Jungle* (1955), both garnered huge economic returns from its teen fan base and established a direct link in the minds of the moral majority between rock'n'roll and teenage violence. In Britain the film was afforded an X certificate and so barred to its depicted audience. Instead, it was Sam Katzman's hastily arranged spinoff *Rock Around the Clock* (1956) that, straight from its UK première on 10 July 1956, occasioned wild behaviour among audiences, with dancing in the aisles and cinema seats torn out. Anthony Bicat illustrated the collapse of civilisation as we knew it: 'In Manchester, after showing *Rock Around the Clock*, ten youths were fined for insulting behaviour when they left the cinema. "Rhythm-crazed" youngsters, after they had seen the film, held up traffic for half an hour and trampled in the flower beds of the municipal gardens.'[4]

More worryingly for the film industry than a few trashed flowers, Bicat reports that 'in Blackburn the Watch Committee banned the film'.[5] Despite the film being passed by the censors, it was likely that local authorities would exercise their prerogative and prohibit further examples of celluloid rock. Even though the film's success led to Haley simultaneously occupying five places in the Top 30 that September, rock'n'roll was just too hot to handle and so, in a pattern echoing the American scenario, the concomitant lack of interest from major British studios gave small independent companies the chance to move in for a potentially quick killing. Sensing a passing phase of limited appeal, they too insisted on a cheap, hastily churned out product and diluted rock with what they judged the more authentically indigenous sounds of skiffle and jazz.

First into the spotlight came *The Tommy Steele Story* (1957), quickly followed by Steele epigone Terry Dene in *The Golden Disc* (1958), while the whole new pop star phenomenon was swiftly ironised in the literate *Expresso Bongo* (1959). This starred Cliff Richard, who had made his feature film debut as a leather-jacketed trouble-maker in *Serious Charge* (1959), set like its predecessors in the amoral environment synonymous with early British rock, the coffee bar. The 'long sixties' witnessed a recurring duality where the young were both celebrated as the harbingers of an exciting and prosperous future and condemned as exemplifying a new moral and cultural bankruptcy. These are key motifs around which dominant interpretations of social change were formulated, and culturally the early British pop musicals can be seen as working to establish these twin tropes, the thesis and anti-thesis of what Dick Hebdige has termed 'youth-as-fun' and 'youth-as-trouble'.[6] Economically, these British pop musicals were largely conceived as exploitation movies, a category defined by John Hill as conventionally low-budget, aimed at specific target audiences and heavily reliant on a quick turnover of capital.[7] In a review of *Beat Girl* (1960), the final member of the coffee bar quintet, the film critic of *The Times* knowingly laid out the plan of attack:

> This is the sort of film that is made to a formula for a market that is eager and anxious for it. The idea is to get a popular singer – in this instance, Mr. Adam Faith – concentrate on the 'beat' generation and the jivers in the cellars, set the action against a background of striptease, clubs and coffee bars, tack a perfunctory moral on the end, and sit back and wait for the click of money at the box-offices.[8]

Though castigated as cynically commercial and flagrantly formulaic, the financial returns were limited – British pop music remained a parochial affair – and its film vehicles were an uncertain mix of musical styles and melodramatic narratives. Only *The Tommy Steele Story* made a significant profit: £100,000 in its opening four months.

Cinema changed in the late 1950s, and so did its music, though in opposite directions. Alongside the ostensibly radical style and content of 'new wave' cinema there came a transmutation of rock'n'roll into more traditional musical forms. Here again there is a two-year watershed: Charlie Gillett sees rock'n'roll as having 'petered out' around 1958, partly because of its recuperation by the music industry,[9] while for Nik Cohn 1960 was rock's *annus horribilis*: 'Everyone had gone to the moon. Elvis had been penned off in the army and came back to appal us with ballads. Little Richard had got religion. Chuck Berry was in jail, Buddy Holly was dead. Very soon, Eddie Cochran was killed in his car crash. It was a wholesale plague, a wipe-out.'[10]

It was Cliff Richard, the star of Britain's one 'new wave' musical, *Expresso Bongo*, who came along to save the day, or give up the ghost, depending on one's viewpoint. 'Rock-pop' is the term used by Dick Bradley to signify the music that emerged from this blending of rock'n'roll and the desire of the industry – and the artists themselves – to expand their sales range.[11] Gillett sees Cliff as one of the prime movers in this transformation[12] while 'Living Doll' is the perfect illustration of this 'rock-pop' hybrid, with its slower beat which, as Cliff knew only too well, 'appealed to parents who had money'.[13]

For some this was a betrayal: George Melly states that 'Richard is the key figure in relation to the castration of the first British pop explosion. Steele may have abandoned pop for show biz but Richard dragged pop into show biz.'[14] However, this absorption of rock'n'roll, its 'recuperation' into the mainstream, can be seen as adding to the form's potential for expansion and development. Cliff's cinema trilogy of the early 1960s, *The Young Ones* (1961), *Summer Holiday* (1962) and *Wonderful Life* (1964), not only illustrate but also enact this process, and provide a more affluent alternative to the exploitation 'quickie'. Others, such as Robert Murphy, approved: 'Despite Richard's limitations as an actor they are lively, inventive, enjoyable films, their young directors Sidney Furie and Peter Yates being more in tune with their subject than the Hollywood veterans entrusted with Elvis Presley's musicals.'[15]

The trajectory of Cliff Richard's film career perfectly dramatised the trend of 'blending' (or gelding) the rock star into more traditional forms of entertainment. In *Serious Charge* he is a coffee bar rocker, a clear sign to an adult audience of juvenile delinquency. By the time of *Wonderful Life* Cliff is a son-in-law to dream for, with any remnants of rock'n'roll now a mere musical accompaniment to beach parties and good clean fun. It is this early 1960s trilogy rather than its coffee bar predecessors that are unflinchingly formulaic. *The Young Ones*, *Summer Holiday* and *Wonderful Life* all have at their centre a clash between Youth and Age, a narrative structure that foregrounds a parent–child conflict, and in each there is a set-piece confrontation where Cliff, spokesman for the younger generation, points out just how efficient and responsible they are. Any members of the older generation who label them as delinquents are themselves shown to be mean-spirited and misguided: eventually they see the error of their ways and realise that the kids are all right.

Sound and image develop together in perfect harmony as the Cliff Richard trilogy displays a musical and moral makeover, a tactic to ease the entry of rock'n'roll singers into the welcoming arms and wealthy pockets of more adult forms of entertainment, above all the variety stage, where slow ballads were more appreciated than a four-chord rocker. Free from the pernicious influences of Brando, Dean and Presley, the British pop musical looked back across the Atlantic to find inspiration from Rooney, Garland and Kelly as Cliff's trilogy strives to employ the styles and structures of the Hollywood musical. All three films are prestigious productions: unusually in a vehicle for a teen idol, they employ colour and a wide-screen format, and ape the Hollywood tradition with energetic dances, choreographed songs and duet numbers between the male and female leads. Each film contains the standard medley section and, eager to pull in all sections of the marketplace, each finds room to include at least one rock'n'roll number.

By doing so, each film inevitably also employs the ideological underpinnings of the Hollywood musical. A genre such as the musical is not just a film type; it brings with it certain spectator expectations, certain structures, codes and conventions which combine in the musical to indicate its function as, in Richard Dyer's phrase, a 'gospel of happiness'.[16] Susan Hayward summarises the ideological strategies of the genre as 'selling marriage, gender fixity, communal stability and the merits of capitalism'.[17] This selling would prove all too easy for Cliff and the Shadows to perform. *The Young Ones* and *Summer Holiday* both proved the second top box-office earner at British cinemas for 1962 and 1963 respectively, and garnered much critical praise. By the time *Wonderful Life* was premièred at the Empire Theatre, Leicester Square, on 2 July 1964, however, the spontaneity and freshness was judged to have gone, the critics mauled the piece and, most significantly, it proved by far the least financially successful of the trio. John Coleman noted a tiredness in the formula, a slipping from the zeitgeist: 'what looked pleasing domestic mateyness in *The Young Ones* now comes over as desperation'.[18] What precipitated this sudden fall from grace? In truth, Cliff's time had passed; there were new kids on the block and the boy from Lucknow, India, together with his traditional pop musicals, were about to be drowned out by the twist and shout emanating from Merseyside.

AN EARLY CLUE TO THE NEW DIRECTION

On Friday 5 October 1962 the Beatles' first single was released in the United Kingdom on the Parlophone label, number R 4949. Although 'Love Me Do' reached only number 17 in the charts, its modest success presaged a seismic shift in an indigenous industry previously dominated by American and British balladeers and London-based groups. With their next single, 'Please Please Me', the group's characteristic sound was established: high-pitched harmonies, Harrison's lead guitar, simple yet effective love lyrics. Though the song made number 1 in only a few charts, beaten to some magazines' top spot by Frank Ifield's 'Wayward Wind', the 'Fab Four' – as the media had already dubbed them – achieved this feat with their next three singles, 'From Me to You', 'She Loves You' and 'I Wanna Hold Your Hand'. By the close of 1963 they were the most popular artists in Britain and Europe, selling not only records but also a new image, with collarless jackets and mop-top hairstyles. The 'youth quake' that had struck America in 1956 with Elvis Presley and rock'n'roll now struck in Western Europe with the Beatles and the 'Merseybeat'.

Initially these shock waves failed to trouble the United States. EMI's American label, Capitol Records, no doubt mindful of the failure of British 'sensations' such as Cliff Richard to make the slightest impact on the US market, were still refusing to issue the Beatles' records and so their first four releases were handled by the tiny independent labels, Swan and Vee-Jay, with a commensurate lack of market 'clout'.

Noel Rodgers, the British representative for United Artists Records, however, was seeing the burgeoning phenomenon of Beatlemania from his London base and was convinced that it would inevitably reach the USA. On discovering that EMI had failed to cover film soundtracks in their contract with the group, Rodgers approached George 'Bud' Ornstein, the production head of United Artists' European film division, with the proposal that they offer the Beatles a three-picture deal in order to obtain three – they hoped lucrative – soundtrack albums. United Artists had opened its European division in 1961 with a brief to produce half a dozen low-budget films a year, and Ornstein had already financed *Dr No* (1962) and *Tom Jones* (1963), British-based products that became box-office successes, especially in the United States. Showing early signs of 'the Midas touch', Ornstein was encouraged to back his instincts. Given Capitol's apparent lack of interest, even he was primarily interested in obtaining the Beatles on record for United Artists and initially had little idea of the films' separate commercial potential. United Artists was expanding its music and recording arm, and here was an opportunity to secure publishing rights for the sheet music and soundtrack album rights. The leaders of the new 'Merseybeat sound' seemed a viable proposition.

Thus, in its conception, the greatest British pop musical was akin, not to the mainstream Cliff-style trilogy, but to the coffee-bar-style musicals before it: a low-budget exploitation movie to milk the latest brief musical craze for all it was worth.

With a cheap and cheerful product in mind, Ornstein approached Walter Shenson, an independent American producer with experience of making low-budget films in Britain. Shenson had moved to Britain to make his first feature, *The Mouse that Roared* (1959), an Ealingesque satire where the tiny Duchy of Grand Fenwick declares war on the United States, confident that losers always win out economically. The film starred Peter Sellers in three key roles and, while doing satisfactory business in England, conquered its on-screen rival, proving a huge success in America. When Shenson turned his thoughts to a sequel, Sellers declined, but recommended a director who, he felt, was very much on the same satirical/slapstick wavelength – Richard Lester.

A child prodigy, Dick Lester went up to university at the age of fifteen and graduated from the University of Pennsylvania with a degree in clinical psychology. Perhaps more influential to his future film career, he was also a gifted musician and, while a student, composed light music and formed a short-lived vocal group. After university Lester became a CBS television floor manager, where he learned to deal with the 'surreal' accidents of live television, mainly by employing as many cameras as possible. He moved on to work as a morning disc jockey, even a puppeteer on Ed Sullivan's *Toast of the Town*. He decided to travel, arrived in England in 1955, toured Europe, and earned his living playing guitar and jazz piano in bars and cafés. On his return to London, the twenty-three-year-old Lester was employed making commercials for the newly created commercial television network and was soon handed the production duties for Associated-Rediffusion-Television's first jazz programme, *Downbeat*, followed by *The Dick Lester Show*, a first attempt to re-create for television the ad-libbed humour typical of the Goons.

Lester's eponymous venture lasted for only one broadcast, but it brought him to the attention of Peter Sellers, also keen to give a visual embodiment to the Goons' surreal humour. With Sellers, Spike Milligan, Michael Bentine and Harry Secombe, Lester made a series of comedy shows, *Idiot's Weekly, Price 2d*, *A Show Called Fred* and *Son of Fred*. More significantly, the partnership almost accidentally produced *The Running, Jumping and Standing Still Film* (1959), shot on two consecutive Sundays in a field in Muswell Hill with a 16mm camera owned by Sellers. This glorified home movie, eleven minutes long and completed at a cost of £70, starred a Fab Four of Sellers, Milligan, Mario Fabrizi and Leo McKern, consisted of Goon-like vignettes of the English at play and had a cool jazz score composed by Lester himself. Sellers, impressed with the result, showed the film to Herbert Kretzmer, television critic of the *Daily Express*, and it was soon on the road to celebrity. Exhibited at the Edinburgh Festival, it won a prize at the San Francisco Film Festival and was subsequently nominated for an Academy Award. Back in England, it was picked up by Roy Boulting for British Lion Films and given a commercial release in the News Theatre, Praed Street. *The Running, Jumping and Standing Still Film* has subsequently drawn comparisons with Buñuel and Vigo,[19] but its importance for the British pop musical was to demonstrate to Goon lovers such as George Martin and the Beatles that an American director was perfectly attuned to English eccentricity and Spike Milligan's nonsensical, irreverent humour.

It was Lester's next project, a return to the *Downbeat* world of jazz, however, that would provide his chance to break into major commercial cinema. His direction of a pilot programme, a thirty-minute mixture of documentary techniques and modern jazz, entitled *Have Jazz, Will Travel*, brought him to the attention of the film producer Milton Subotsky. Subotsky, known for giving young talent its chance, thought that Lester, having shown confidence and innovation in filming musicians, would be a good choice to direct his latest project, an exploitation pop musical centred on the new trad jazz craze. It is reported that Subotsky initially mailed Lester twenty pages of notes. As Lester told Roy Carr: 'I read them and said, "I think I can do something with this. I have a few ideas. As soon as you have the first draft of the script send it to me."'[20] Lester was promptly told that what he had just read was the complete shooting script. The storyline, as everybody realised, was just a pretext to fit in twenty-plus musical numbers in the allotted time. Lester agreed to the assignment, his first opportunity to direct a major cinema feature, and set to work for the British arm of Columbia Pictures.

It's Trad, Dad! is musically interesting as an unconsciously valedictory snapshot of the state of British popular music in that doldrums period between the original 1950s rock and the Beatles, a more placid time where youth, with a tamed Cliff Richard as its cinematic spokesman, knew its place. Starring 'school-girl singing sensation' Helen Shapiro and 'boy next door' Craig Douglas, a roll-call stretching from the 'twister' Chubby Checker to the Edwardian pastiche of the Temperance Seven shows the total lack of direction that came to define the 1961–62 period. Shot over a three-week period with a budget of £50,000, *It's Trad, Dad!* is not primarily a film showcasing trad jazz. Instead it reveals a 'buckshot' technique, aiming at a vast range of targets in the hope that something worthwhile would eventually be hit.

To gain sufficient footage with almost no plot and a negligible shooting schedule allowing little time for retakes, Lester drew on his experiences when working on American television. Neil Sinyard tells how Lester opted to shoot with multiple cameras, a technique born of necessity but one that proved so successful he continued with it thereafter. 'The shooting strategy consisted of having three cameras filming each musical number three times, giving the director a variety of visual and editing possibilities.'[21] This procedure allowed for speed and security, a 'live' feel to the musical numbers, and facilitated the staccato rhythm of editing Lester preferred to employ.

Significantly this is also the first time in a British pop musical that television is seen not as the enemy but as the ally of cinematic advances (though in time it would prove itself the pop musical's nemesis). As Alexander Walker observes, '*It's Trad, Dad!* was the first feature film that successfully made the presentation techniques of television commercials and the pop shows on the small screen designed for the teenage and sub-teenage audiences into an integral part of its jokey structure.'[22] Here above all is where Lester's television apprenticeship comes to the fore. Producers and directors working in television were, for the most part, considerably younger than those who worked in the cinema industry, and they brought a new ingredient to the visual presentation of pop music: speed. This was integral to the BBC's early-evening mix of skiffle, rock and trad jazz, *6.5 Special*. Its producer, Jack Good, who would later create *Wham!* and *Oh Boy!* for the commercial network is, for Walker, central to this new visual correlative. 'Jack Good ... did more than anyone else to invent the pop style on the box in which pop personalities were marketed with the same ingenuity as the goods in the commercials.'[23] *It's Trad, Dad!* is the first British pop musical to utilise the 'good grammar' of television's techniques and its audience's expectations.

Walker is right to note how the film 'moved at the speed of the hard-sell merchandising',[24] but added to the commercial efficiency was an ability to layer on eye-catching effects taken from the contemporary practices of both art and commerce. Lester possessed a sensibility well attuned to musical presentation, and could 'instinctively' match if not enhance the performer's skills with a concomitant virtuosity in direction, photography and editing. Here, for the first time in a British pop musical, the grammar of cinematic correlation seems both artistically appropriate and empathetic.

For example, of the opening number with Terry Lightfoot and his New Orleans Jazzmen performing 'Tavern in the Town', Neil Sinyard comments that the screen is 'sectionalised for visual variety and virtuosity'.[25] It also makes the audience focus on each new patch of image as it appears, which serves the function of allowing a full introduction to every member of the band. First at the top of the screen centre we see Lightfoot on the clarinet, then a small square screen right presents the drums. A third square far left draws our attention to the banjo. Then, added to Lightfoot in an inverted T, come the trumpet and trombone. The double bass, low right, completes the line-up and opens out the whole screen. Thus, instead of focusing only on the leader, Lightfoot, this 'virtuoso' technique brings all members of the band to our attention. Music is a communal activity: the 'democratic' sectional editing honours that interdependence.

Lester is equally adept at presenting pop performers. For Gene Vincent, abandoning his classic black leathers and hard rock sound on 'Spaceship to Mars', the clip begins with a close-up of the neck of a guitar screen left, the neck of a saxophone screen right, while between them, out of focus, is the white shape of Vincent, almost indistinguishable against the white background. The song that follows sees a constant interplay of form and focus between the singer and the stylistic polarities of rock guitar and jazz saxophone, with Vincent mostly small and distant, an uncertain player in a tentative song of jazz–rock fusion. In contrast to this visual diffidence Del Shannon's 'She Never Talked About Me' is filmed largely through fetishising close-ups, sometimes extreme close-ups that fill the screen with Shannon's mouth and chin or face from the eyes up: the song's self-obsessed lyrics perfectly matched by the visual framing.

Above all, the film displays a knowledge of the processes of musical performance. John Leyton's 'Lonely City' is introduced by a shot of the singer seen through a circular window like a disc. Helen Shapiro's ardour mists up the window, delaying a focused appearance of the film's 'special guest star'. But when we cut through into the recording studio, Leyton remains behind glass, isolated in a small booth. As he sings we see the reflection of a string section in the glass; they are engaged in a group activity but Leyton remains separated, the pop star lonely amid the crowd. The romantic lyric is undercut by Leyton flipping over the music and taking a few quick drags on a cigarette between verses, so that a sense of boredom seeps into the recording experience. It is the film's first insight into the *routine* of the job, even for chart-topping singing stars.

Alongside inside knowledge of the industry, Lester knowingly employs the devices of op and pop art. For instance, Acker Bilk's number 'Frankie and Johnny' is filmed with a wire mesh placed in front of the camera. This gives the impression, as contemporary reviewers noted, 'either of news photos or Lichtenstein prints'.[26] The film itself is aware that it is dealing with a transient phenomenon, and emphasises the point at both structural and visual levels. The sheer number of performers, each receiving a maximum of a couple of minutes, some having their performances overlaid with plot dialogue, gives a sense of the here-today-gone-tomorrow nature of the musicians and their wares. The film's closing titles are presented in the form of grainy newspaper photographs, again an ambiguous summation: the performers are frozen in perpetuity but are also soon to be yesterday's news (as in truth a number of these artists already were). This last point is reinforced when, during the final number, the camera highlights a dancing girl trampling all over a newspaper on the floor: a visual comment on the insubstantial nature of pop fame. That this dance is to a saxophone solo in a distinctly modern jazz idiom, courtesy of Sounds Inc., only adds to the idea that the film is aware that it is already a historical document.

Alongside the innovative *mise-en-scène*, the key ingredient of *It's Trad, Dad!* is its humour. With so many musical numbers to cram in, the film has little time to exploit comedy of situation or of character; the negligible plot concerns the efforts of Helen Shapiro and friends to organise a music concert to save their coffee bar from the bureaucracy of the mayor and his cronies. Instead, it is packed with visual gags, many of them straight from the Goon school, with speeded-up film – the parents at a buffet; stills – Acker Bilk and his band dashing for a cup of tea; and captions – arrows pointing out 'Boy', 'Girl' and 'Mayor' from a crowd scene. It demonstrates Lester's respect for the visual inventiveness of silent cinema, and is coupled with a disregard for linear narrative. From the outset Lester stands at an oblique angle to the fledgling pop musical genre, setting up a knowingly playful discussion with his material and audience. This playfulness is not patronising, precisely because Lester makes a positive virtue of his young leads' inexperience and idealism.

When Helen and Craig need help organising a concert to save their beloved coffee bar – as ever doing the show right here – the narrator facilitates travel by removing the film background, leaving the leads momentarily against a plain white screen, before inserting a new piece of film that places them in the corridors of the BBC and permits the plot to speed on. Much of this is ludic before elucidatory, a collusive play with cinematic technique and generic convention, though it also acts as a distancing device, precluding a coherent worldview and pressing the viewer to question the cinematic experience – a standard Brechtian device. Other comic elements signify thematically. For example, while looking for a disc jockey at the BBC, Helen and Craig enter the music department, only to find musicians stacked on shelves, waiting for their call. Again, this works as a device for Lester's reduction to absurdity of the film's diegetic world, though metaphorical interpretations are also possible: the utilitarian manner in which the corporation hires and fires musicians with scant regard to continuity of labour; the inevitable boredom and hanging around consistent with the profession.

Again of thematic interest for Lester's later film musicals, there is the constant axis of generational conflict. Alexander Walker notes how the very title serves notice of discord: 'The words "trad" and "dad" in the title had the flip, mocking emphasis of a generation growing more aggressively conscious almost daily of their own identity and creating heroes who were certainly not those of their fathers.'[27] Yet an inclusive ambiguity is equally present: the titular rhyme can also suggest a generational compatibility, the recuperation of the music from a previous decade as one's own, *and* the appropriation of that new trend by the older generation. When the teenage jazz fans succeed in avoiding adult roadblocks and their televised concert begins, Helen tells the journalist to go over and flatter the mayor's ego. The musical event is, short-term, a victory for the young, but the mayor's hypocritical acquiescence suggests how easily new cultures can be appropriated by the dominant ideology. As such the film's ending can be more cynically read as indicating how politicians were coming to realise the merits of media presentation: it is certainly an astute anticipation of Harold Wilson sharing 'purple heart' jokes with the Beatles at the Annual Variety Club of Great Britain Awards on 19 March 1964.

It's Trad, Dad! impressed the critics with its energy and visual flair. Accorded twenty words by Dilys Powell, doyenne of *The Sunday Times* since the 1940s, her summary highlighted 'jazz for the tweenagers, deafening, orgiastic and dashingly shot'.[28] Isabel Quigly also noted 'quite a bit of ear-splitting charm' and 'the director actually varying his techniques to suit those of the performers he's filming'.[29] These were indicative of the general trend: the music's decibel-enhanced drive being varyingly patronised or pilloried, but the film-maker's 'tricks' receiving plaudits. David Robinson wrote of Lester betraying 'a tyro's immoderate interest in technical tricks' but readily admitted that 'it is all done with such frank enjoyment and at such a determined pace that criticism is disarmed'.[30]

Within the industry criticism was also disarmed by the film's clear commercial success: *It's Trad, Dad!* recouped its costs six times over in Britain alone. Alone, since its returns abroad proved slight, even in the United States. Nevertheless, Lester was clearly bankable and he followed *It's Trad, Dad!* with *The Mouse on the Moon* (1963), a Sellers-less and inferior sequel to *The Mouse that Roared*, with the Duchy of Grand Fenwick now beating the superpowers in the space race. Lester here had much less freedom with casting or with material, but he still fashioned a financial success on both sides of the Atlantic, and the start of a fruitful partnership between director and producer.

With his two *Mouse* movies Walter Shenson had shown himself in possession of the knack of making British product accessible to the US market: thus he was a logical figure for Ornstein to approach. As Shenson later revealed, Ornstein's brief was simple: to make a film 'with enough new songs by the Beatles for a new album'.[31] Indeed, given their lack of interest in the film itself, United Artists were almost willing to give it away. It is reported that when the meeting to discuss the deal was arranged with Brian Epstein in October 1963, Ornstein and Shenson had privately agreed that they would be prepared to give the Beatles 25 per cent of the net profits. They were surprised when Epstein said immediately that he would not consider anything under 7.5 per cent net, plus £20,000. Ornstein shook hands on the deal – and then faced the problem of selling the issue to head office: for all his earlier success, spy and literary genres had some past record of international success, but no previous British pop musical had made any mark in the States. Even with the group's star constantly in the ascendant, there was little intrinsic or archival interest in the celluloid side-product: United Artists' sole concern was that the Beatles produce original material for the soundtrack, and promotional posters subsequently plugged heavily the fact that the film contained '6 Brand New Songs plus your Beatles Favorites!' A standard low-budget ceiling of £200,000 was agreed, with film rights to return to Shenson after fifteen years.

JUST GOOD FRIENDS

Epstein had been easy to persuade; it would prove much harder to convince the Fab Four that a three-film project would be a sound career move. After all, they had proven themselves as performers and songwriters. Why risk a medium where none of them had any experience? The example of other pop stars was also less than inspiring. Roy Carr quotes from John Lennon:

> We'd made it clear to Brian that we weren't interested in being stuck in one of those typical nobody-understands-our-music plots where the local dignitaries are trying to ban something as terrible as the Saturday-night hop. The kind of thing where we'd just pop up a couple of times between the action ... all smiles and clean shirt collars to sing our latest record and once again at the end when the local mayor has been convinced that we're not all mass-murderers or, worse still, about to start shagging some young Sunday school teacher in the town hall flower beds ... We all know that scene so well ... where he and a bunch of senile town councillors and the police chief start dancing around all over the place like those bloody *Thunderbirds* puppets ... Never mind all your pals, how could we have faced each other if we had allowed ourselves to be involved in that kind of movie?[32]

Given that the above retrospective analysis includes (if one omits the shagging) an almost perfect plot summary of *It's Trad, Dad!*, it might seem perverse that Shenson's selection to direct John, Paul, George and Ringo would be that very film's director: Dick, now Richard, Lester. One could see why Shenson himself would be comfortable with the choice: the two men had a proven working relationship in financial and suitable generic terms. *It's Trad, Dad!* was known to the Beatles, mainly because of the appearance of Gene Vincent, whom the group had befriended during their time at the Cavern Club, but it was to be his earliest work that won Lester the group's approval. Roy Carr quotes Paul McCartney on the choice of director:

> We discussed this with Brian on a number of occasions and he asked if we had any ideas of our own. The only person we could think of was, whoever made that *Running, Jumping and Standing Still Film*? Who did that, 'cause it was brilliant? The thing was, we all really loved that Goons film so, right away, that was an indication of the kind of direction we were all interested in ... Basically, it was just what we liked. We could relate to the humour wholeheartedly. Brian discovered

that it had been made by Richard Lester and so we said, 'Well he's all right by us ... we're really up for this one!'[33]

Wherever the initiative lay (and critical consensus weighs against McCartney), Lester was unanimously accepted to direct the Beatles at the tender age of thirty-two, a striking contrast with the average age of those involved in Hollywood youth pictures, calculated by Robin Bean at 65.6.[34] Alongside him, the thirty-eight-year-old George Martin was, logically, appointed musical director. He would provide instrumental versions for the film of four Lennon and McCartney compositions: 'This Boy', 'I Should Have Known Better', 'And I Love Her' and 'A Hard Day's Night'.

With sound and vision agreeable to all, next came the vexed issue of finding a suitable screenwriter. Lester's original choice was *'Til Death Do Us Part* creator Johnny Speight, but prior commitments prevented the London-based writer from accepting the commission. Instead, the 'professional Liverpudlian' Alun Owen was chosen, though again the instigation is unclear, it being either at the behest of Lester or McCartney, depending on the sources consulted. ('Walter Shenson says it was Paul who suggested Alun Owen as the scriptwriter for the Beatles' first film';[35] Lester said, 'I felt that I could persuade the Beatles that he could write for them').[36] Alun Owen was born in North Wales in 1926 and spoke only Welsh until he went to school, moving to Liverpool with his parents at the age of eight. His first performed piece was a radio play, *Two Sons*, broadcast early in 1958, while his stage plays *The Rough and Ready Lot* and *Progress to the Park* followed the next year. The former quickly transferred from the Royal Court to an extended run at Joan Littlewood's Theatre Royal, Stratford East and then on to the West End. Commissioned by Sydney Newman to write for his newly formed Armchair Theatre slot on the BBC, Owen drew particular praise for his television dramas with a Northern setting. *After the Funeral*, *Lena*, *O My Lena* and *No Trams to Lime Street* were produced for the series within a year, and earned Owen the award of 'TV Playwright of 1959–60'. (George Melly would later dub him 'the first poet of television drama'.)[37] Among subsequent television work, he worked with Lester on the short-lived *Dick Lester Show* and, when approached by Brian Epstein, was cutting his musical teeth by working on the book for Lionel Bart's upcoming Merseyside musical, *Maggie May*. (Plans for a film version starring Peter Sellers would later fall through.)

First, though, Owen had to hope he passed the audition, spending a few days with the Beatles to see if they got along and he got their style. Paul McCartney recalled:

> He wasn't too above us and pretty soon we felt that he was starting to get the idea of what we were about. The important thing is that Owen didn't attempt to turn us into characters that we weren't. Those parts of the film where they did, just didn't work and they ended up on the cutting room floor. The secret to the success of *A Hard Day's Night* was that there was a little of our own personalities in it.[38]

That 'secret to the success' had already been decided by October 1963, during the weekend following their appearance on *Sunday Night at the London Palladium* – the single moment that is acknowledged to have heralded the start of Beatlemania. Shenson recalls that the idea struck him when he first met the group to discuss a film deal, in a cramped taxi ride to a recording studio in London. It was there and then that he observed their nervous, captive energy.[39] According to Lester, though, the idea came from – or perhaps crystallised around – a reply John made when asked about a trip they had made to Sweden. 'Ooh, it was a room and a car, and a car and a room, and a room and a car,' he said.[40]

A fictionalised documentary of the group's real-life relationship to fame called for black-and-white photography to replicate the footage flooding television screens, newspapers and magazines. Owen felt this format especially appropriate as it also suited the quartet's personalities: 'Getting to know them was remarkably easy,' he said. 'They are immediate people and I knew from that that it couldn't be a colour film. The boys are essentially black-and-white people.'[41] Perhaps the public here bleeds into the personal, since Owen's previous experience of the Beatles' image, like everyone else's, had been almost exclusively black-and-white. As Mike Evans noted, 'Whereas most pop acts "put up" with monochrome until they could afford the dubious luxury of the Cliff Richard Technicolor record sleeve style of pictures, the Beatles' photographs consistently exploited the black-and-white medium for its own sake.'[42] Running through from the Hamburg pictures of Jurgen Vollmer and Astrid Kirchherr to the posed fan photos of Les Chadwick, and peaking with *A Hard Day's Night*, there was a common 'grainy' black-and-white realisation that became a dominant feature of the Beatles' image for years to come. Whatever the precise moment of inspiration for the film's main theme, Owen's brief, once accepted

1. 'From Me to You'. A film awash with images of the Beatles, 'black-and-white people'.

by the boys, was to write an exaggerated day in their life, and he was dispatched to Dublin in early November to witness at first hand the group's increasingly chaotic tour schedule. He began the script there and then, and dropped in again to see them in Paris while they were staying at the George V Hotel in mid-January. The first draft was ready by late January 1964.

Ornstein claims that he 'fell in love' with Owen's script – which was fortunate with only five weeks left to shooting. He did, though, challenge one sequence. Set in a second-hand clothes store, Ringo struck up a conversation with the 'typically Jewish' proprietor, before taking over behind the counter to sell a top hat and coat to East Indian sailors, portrayed, according to Ornstein, as 'stupid niggers'. (In the finished film we merely see Ringo enter a second-hand clothes shop and re-emerge immediately in disguise.) Instead, Owen wrote what many considered one of the best scenes in the film, where Ringo meets a group of truant schoolkids.

The short, staccato nature of Owen's script was particularly favoured by all concerned. Practically it meant that the Beatles had to speak only one sentence at a time: thus the inexperienced actors could literally learn their lines one at a time, or even repeat after Lester the required inflection and expression. This 'fragmented' style also fitted well with a broader strategy: to emphasise the distinct personalities of the Fab Four by devising separate sequences where each would act on

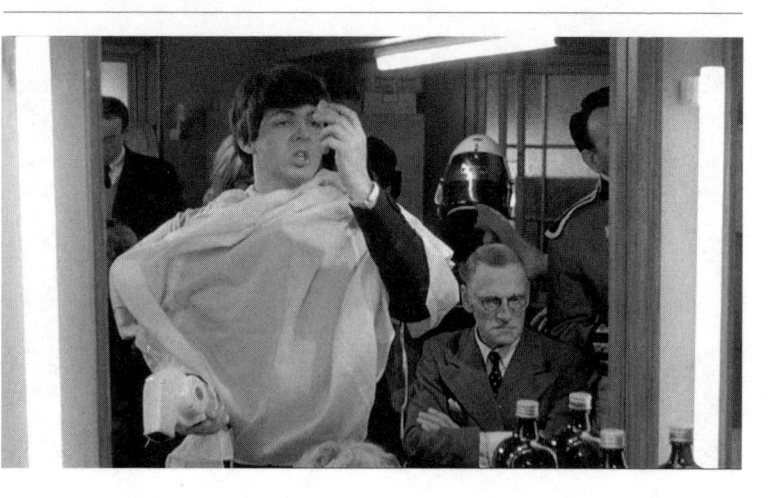

2. *'Powdered Gee-gaws'. Paul as actor: a bit of Shakespeare that did not hit the cutting-room floor.*

his own. Thus Ringo exchanged a clothes store and racial stereotypes for a canal bank and bunking children; George was interrogated by a designer of teenage fashion; John interacted with a woman backstage who recognised his face but couldn't put a name to it.

The exception is Paul, whose 'solo' scene, shot at the Jack Billings TV School of Dancing, Goldhawk Road, was later cut from the film. The scene began with Paul searching for an errant Ringo and coming across an old church hall bearing the sign 'TV Rehearsal Room'. He ventures inside and notices a girl, Isla Blair, dressed in theatrical costume and walking about the large room quoting Shakespeare. After a while she notices Paul and stops her speech. Paul asks her to continue, but she tells him to leave as he is spoiling her rehearsal. He remains and they start talking about acting. Paul tells her that he would approach her part in the manner of 'a Liverpool scrubber': his down-to-earth way of explaining the character with which she is grappling. He remembers he has to find Ringo and says farewell, but as he leaves he hears the actress resume in her earlier artificial, actorly tones before pausing and switching to a more naturalistic manner of speech, just as Paul had proposed.

Opting for the natural and Northern, the scene encapsulates the *modus operandi* of the entire film; despite taking up two whole days of their busy shooting schedule, however, it failed to make the final cut, ostensibly because it failed to achieve the naturalness it advocated.

For Lester it was partly a case of Paul's delivery: 'At that time he was probably the most self-conscious actor because he knew more about acting than the others. He had a girlfriend who was an actress [Jane Asher] and he was a regular visitor to the theatre. He had more to lose because he had probably thought about it a bit more.'[43] For McCartney, it was the situation itself: 'I had to sort of wander around her with the camera going round and round in circles ... all very Sixties, all very French and I had to repeat these very quirky lines. We had a whole day of doing that, but it didn't work because it wasn't the kind of thing we would have done in everyday life ... It was all a little bit too contrived.'[44]

By mid-February 1964, though, everyday life for the Beatles had changed – dramatically. It constitutes the greatest pop story ever told. With 'I Wanna Hold Your Hand' finally granted a full release by Capitol, the Beatles had become permanent fixtures on American airwaves. They had wowed the press the moment their Pan Am flight touched down at New York's John F. Kennedy International Airport on 7 February; two nights later they had been seen on the *Ed Sullivan Show* – by the highest viewing figures ever for a television broadcast (73 million people in over 23 million homes) – and in the space of just two weeks proceeded to conquer the hearts and pockets of America. The richest nation had been shaken out of its post-Kennedy mourning; the home of rock'n'roll had finally succumbed to 'the British invasion'. With their mop-tops known from coast to coast and their full back-catalogue about to occupy every spot in the Billboard Top 5 – a neat reversal of Bill Haley's earlier UK monopoly – the Beatles had become, almost overnight, the most bankable pop stars on the planet. And they were due to start working with Richard Lester on a rock-bottom-financed exploitation quickie in ten days' time.

With an entirely different bargaining position now at his disposal, Ornstein rapidly called for talks with Epstein, Shenson and Lester. Unsurprisingly, the group's lawyer David Jacobs renegotiated their contract up from 7.5 per cent to equal Shenson's 30 per cent of net profits (United Artists as financier and distributor took the remaining 40 per cent)[45] but all parties were of a mind not to alter any more of the existing arrangements for the Beatles' first movie. For a start, the shooting schedule was extremely tight – a première date had been set for July, with shooting due to begin in March. Second, there was a limit to what a fuller budget could add to the 'faux-documentary' filming style that

Lester and Shenson had decided on: more money would only mean more film footage, and therefore more editing, and more time wasted. They were certain that they did not want to change the film to colour.

There was one change, however, that all deemed politic. Following the enormous success of the Beatles' press conference at Kennedy Airport, Owen was asked to include a scene that would allow the boys to shine in a similar fashion. He therefore added a press buffet in a theatre lounge, a scene that demonstrates the enjoyment and entrapment of the quartet. Structurally, Owen wrote the scene not like New York but in the pattern of a reception the group attended at the British Embassy in Washington, DC, on 11 February, when the patronising questioning – and the impromptu, unauthorised cutting of a lock of Ringo's hair – had occasioned the group to walk out. Practically, this London re-creation illustrates concisely the quasi-spontaneous nature of the filming process: Owen's script was tightly plotted, but allowed space for the Beatles to improvise – Shenson and Owen were afraid that their Scouse wit would be blunted by over-rehearsed dialogue. In this scene, as Alexander Walker observes, 'The Beatles improvised jokey, "unphoney" answers to Owen's scripted questions which were sprung on them without forewarning. As with so much else in the film, the skill lay in pitchforking the Beatles into situations they had met many times – then standing back and viewing them that little bit obliquely or oddly.'[46] And fictitiously, since one or two Q+A sequences were later realigned on the editing table to accentuate the bizarre. 'Have you any hobbies?' 'No, actually we're just good friends.'

With speed of the essence, not much time was spent negotiating with agents to gather a cast and crew for the movie. According to Bill Harry, the teenage daughter of a friend told Shenson: 'I'm just praying there'll be no love interest in your Beatles film!'[47] He took the girl's advice and adopted the ploy of all the pre-Cliff British musicals by excluding any romantic ties for the pop star leading men. Thus (ignoring Lennon's recent marriage, as did all branches of the publicity machine) the film bolstered the fantasy feeding Beatlemania, that these four fab guys were still available to all of their adoring fans. Shenson also eschewed big-name stars – a sensible strategy given the modest budget – and awarded the largest non-Beatle part to Wilfrid Brambell, best known for his leading role in the BBC comedy *Steptoe and Son* (1962–74) – later remade in the States as *Sanford and Son* (1972–77). The key was to assemble an experienced team who could be relied upon to deliver the 'tight' script while most attention went into directing the new boys – or reining in their off-the-cuff comments. The boys were helped to 'feel at home' by the casting of Liverpudlian actors Norman Rossington as Norm, the group's road manager, a role loosely based on the travails of real-life equivalent Neil Aspinall, and Deryck Guyler – the narrator in *It's Trad, Dad!* – who played a police sergeant. Actor John Junkin played the group's second road manager, Shake, his role (though not accent or appearance) inspired by the real-life labours of Mal Evans, while Derek Nimmo, who in *It's Trad, Dad!* had played a waiter skilled in prestidigitation, was hired to reprise his role, this time as a straight magician. Kenneth Haigh, who played the part of Simon, an advertising executive, accepted his cheque but, heedless of the message in Paul's cut scene, refused to have his name put in the credits, fearing a low-grade exploitation musical would tarnish his reputation as a Shakespearean actor. (He would, though, star in Bart and Owen's musical *Maggie May* in August 1964.) Victor Spinetti was cast as a manic television director – a successful piece of casting, as he would bond with the group and appear in further Beatles projects. Anna Quayle appeared as studio worker Millie, and a touch of glamour was added with the casting of the 1961 Miss World, Rosemarie Frankland, as a showgirl. Also, there were four schoolgirls featured in an early scene; among them model Patti Boyd, a regular on Lester's early Smith's Crisps TV ads before he rehired her for the Beatles' movie. George Harrison was instantly smitten and a real-life romance began, culminating in marriage – a knowledge of which compensates for the lack of overt love interest on-screen.

Behind the camera were personnel known both to the young director and his stars. With Lester came Gilbert Taylor, in the business since the late 1940s, cameraman on *It's Trad, Dad!* and attuned to the director's artistic vision and working methods. Robert Freeman, the Beatles' semi-official photographer, was commissioned to provide the cover for the soundtrack album – he shot all album covers from *With the Beatles* to *Rubber Soul* – though he also hung around the set taking publicity stills and ended up designing the film's closing credits and film poster. Elsewhere, with spring constituting the low season for the industry, freelance film crews were brought in at modest fees: editor John Jympson had experience of pop musicals from Tommy Steele's *It's All Happening* (1963); art director Ray Simm had worked on 'new wave' product such as *The L-Shaped Room* (1962) and the Tony Newley pop musical *Jazz Boat* (1960); Julie Harris had a career as costume designer dating back to the 1940s and had dressed stars such as Lauren Bacall.

These were 'top flight people for bottom flight money', as associate producer Denis O'Dell would proudly recall.[48]

At the outset, the film also lacked a title. Among the many suggested were: *What Little Old Man?*, one of the first sentences uttered in the film; *Beatlemania*, a term which, by then, was synonymous with any appearance by the quartet; *It's a Daft, Daft, Daft, Daft, World*, a play on Stanley Kramer's contrastingly star-studded 'comedy to end all comedies' of the previous year; plus other names all reflecting the picaresque nature of the project: *Travelling On, Moving On* and *Let's Go*. Reports at the time all claimed that the eventual title *A Hard Day's Night* had come from Ringo, complaining about working into the early hours. The phrase caught on among the group and later, in a brainstorming session to find a suitable name, they repeated Ringo's 'malapropism'. Apparently, on the spot Ornstein declared, 'We just got our title.'[49] In John Lennon's first book *In His Own Write*, published on 23 March 1964, however, there is a story called 'Sad Michael' in which John wrote: 'He'd had a hard day's night that day, for Michael was a Cocky Watchtower.'[50] Ringo, perhaps, had been quoting John: an intertextuality worthy of the finished product.

A YOUNG MAN'S MEDIUM

As with *It's Trad, Dad!*, Lester's new pop film was motivated as a definite hard-sell product, with alacrity essential for the filming process as much as in the final product: shooting began on 2 March, and had to be completed for the Royal Première on 6 July. Speed was certainly a quality that the Beatles possessed in abundance, as evidenced by their build-up to the film. The group returned from their landslide victory in America on Saturday 22 February. The next day they recorded songs and comedy sketches for transmission on *Big Night Out* the following weekend. They took Monday off, and on Tuesday, 25 February reconvened at Abbey Road studios for three days' concentrated recording. The task facing them was to sort out material for the soundtrack of the movie they were to begin shooting in exactly one week's time. In the event, the group took advantage of a provisional extra booking for the evening of 1 March, but as filming began the Beatles were able to hand over to Lester the tapes for nine songs, from which he chose 'Can't Buy Me Love', 'I Should Have Known Better', 'If I Fell', 'I'm Happy Just to Dance with You', 'And I Love Her', 'Tell Me Why' and 'You Can't Do That'.

The recording of the song 'A Hard Day's Night' did not occur until 16 April, as it was only when the title for the film was confirmed that John and Paul were asked to write a song to match it. This was the first time that the duo had been specifically 'commissioned' to write a song: John, adding weight to the notion that the phrase was his initial conception, completed the song that evening. The film was probably named on 13 April, so the song was written that night, was played to Shenson the next morning and recorded two days later – another clear example of the speed at which they were working. With the basic plot already worked out, Lester had nowhere in the film to put the new song: he therefore used it over the opening credit sequence and again at the end. The first two days in June were given over to recording the remaining non-soundtrack material for the British version of *A Hard Day's Night*, making it the only Beatles album to feature exclusively Lennon and McCartney compositions.

This focus and finesse confirms the Beatles' confidence in matters musical. There must, though, have been a pervasive nervousness when, on the morning of Monday, 2 March, all parties convened at Paddington Station, London, to begin filming their yet untitled project. The group had seen the script for the first time only two days previously, and their feeling of entering unknown territory must have been confirmed by their first action of the morning, a hurried entry to the actors' union Equity, proposed and seconded by Brambell and Rossington. Then, at 8.30, the whistle blew and the specially hired train left platform 5 bound for the West Country, with John, Paul, George and Ringo, and the entire filming crew on board. For the first three days the destination was Minehead (on the Wednesday the boys' goading of the snooty Richard Vernon character by running along the platform was shot at the station in Crowcombe, Somerset). For the next two days the train headed for Taunton, and the following Monday made it to Newton Abbot. The cramped environment of train corridors and compartments helped immediately engender an esprit de corps and to create the desired claustrophobia, though from the outset the hoards of hysterical fans left in the group's wake enhanced the reality of restriction. This rather interfered with production schedules (after the first day's pandemonium the group took to boarding the train more secretively, at Acton main line station in West London, and to disembarking prior to Paddington at suburban stations such as West Ealing and Westbourne Park), but for Lester, with his experience in live television broadcasting, it was all suitable raw material. In one scene, for instance, he turned the cameras

3. *'Real Love'. Enjoyment in entrapment (and a glaring continuity error in John's attire).*

on a bunch of screaming girls who had broken through a security barrier and surrounded the Beatles' chauffeur-driven limo after a long day's shooting. This footage was then woven into the film, which explains a continuity error, the boys wearing different clothing on and then off the train. Thus, at times, the fictional documentary became factual – or vice versa.

On Tuesday, 10 March part of Ringo's solo venture was shot at the Turk's Head pub, Winchester Road, within staggering distance of the Twickenham Studios, St Margaret's, Middlesex, where cast and crew met up the next morning to begin the interior shooting. This first day's studio filming constituted more of the same, however, since a set resembling a guard's van was used for the song 'I Should Have Known Better' and later edited into the film's train sequences. All were soon on their travels again, as the Friday saw them move down to Gatwick Airport South, Surrey, to film the closing helicopter departure and the group cavorting on a nearby helicopter launch pad. This was intercut with scenes shot on Thursday, 23 April at the Thornbury playing fields in Isleworth, Middlesex, while the fire escape they scamper down was situated at the back of the Hammersmith Odeon, filmed the previous day. The Ambassadeurs, a private club just off Park Lane, was used on Tuesday, 17 March to film Grandfather gambling; it was revisited on 17 April for the discotheque sequences in the club's Garrison Room. On Monday, 23 March filming switched for seven working days to the Scala

Theatre, Charlotte Street. This was the setting for the group's rehearsals and performance before a live television audience. The climactic performance was filmed on Tuesday, 31 March before an audience of 350 screaming fans, including a thirteen-year-old Phil Collins. Again fact and fiction intermingle: Phil and 250 other drama school children were shipped in (and paid a union rate of £7.50) but, apart from some crowd shots when four extras were sent out on stage dressed up as the Beatles, little acting talent was needed. (The extent of hysterical screaming apparently caused an auditorium-based cameraman's fillings to loosen.) The press party was filmed at the Scala on Thursday, 2 April, hastily arranged in the upstairs bar with a number of real journalists when fan pressure cancelled an outdoor shoot. Indeed, to avoid the persistent problems of Beatlemania, the opening sequence of *A Hard Day's Night* was filmed at nearby Marylebone Station on two Sundays, 5 and 12 April (the sole working weekends of the shooting schedule since the terminus was closed to the public only on Sundays); the film's opening scene, with John, George and Ringo escaping their fans, was shot on the first Sunday at the adjacent Boston Place. The scenes of an allegedly hungover Ringo wandering solo and riverside were filmed on the Thames towpath at Kew on Thursday, 9 April, while George's moments in the spotlight, trashing shirts and teaching shaving, were completed on Monday, 13 April. On 16 April the police station sequences were shot in and around the Clarendon Road in Notting Hill Gate (symbolic of the film's underlying innocence, the police station was actually St John's Secondary School); that same day Ringo was filmed photographing on the Lancaster Road and finding a disguise on the All Saints Road. Paul's aborted solo sequence followed on 20–21 April and filming finished on the morning of 24 April with Ringo failing as Walter Raleigh on a building site on the Edgehill Road, before all reconvened at the Turk's Head for an end-of-film celebration.

A variety of locations, as well as reflecting the Beatles' peripatetic lifestyle, had quickly become a logistical necessity and a large part of the budget was reputedly spent avoiding the crush of fans. 'The biggest problem in making *A Hard Day's Night* on location was that we could, at best, get two takes on anything when we were on a street,' Lester told Ray Coleman. 'The streets would get so blocked with fans we'd have to change locations and start again. We had to get the Beatles on and off the set very quickly!'[51] This quickness in filming also affected both choice of songs and the manner of their cinematic illustration. Of the numbers handed over by Lennon and McCartney, 'I Call Your Name' and their version of Little Richard's 'Long Tall Sally' were immediately dropped, but 'You Can't Do That' hit the cutting-room floor only when Lester's ambitious, off-the-cuff attempt to use ordinary cameras to shoot a stop-motion sequence featuring the Lionel Blair Dancers on stage with the Beatles failed to deliver the required special effects. Elsewhere, though, Lester's ability to recruit chance events into the film would lead to magisterial results, none more so than in the filming of the now famous sequence that would accompany 'Can't Buy Me Love'. As photographer Gilbert Taylor related to Alexander Walker:

> Unfortunately when we came to do a shot from the helicopter, the battery I was handed for the hand-held camera wasn't fully charged – we started the shot and the speed went down. I was able to correct it and by managing to 'stop down' we finished shooting at four frames. I didn't tell Dick till we finished and then I said, 'We shot this in accelerated motion.' His face fell, but when he had the rushes screened it was so successful that we shot a complementary sequence in slow motion.[52]

Thus, what can be seen as the emotional centre of *A Hard Day's Night*, the one time the boys joyfully escape the pressures of fan worship, was initially a mistake: Lester had the skill and daring to make it into a success.

This is not, of course, to attribute all to luck. Elsewhere, Lester now had the confidence – and cheap labour – to increase his trusted method of concurrent filming from multiple angles. For the sequences of the Beatles concert, another *tour de force* of *mise-en-scène* and editing, he employed no fewer than six cameras shooting simultaneously as the Beatles perform. The subsequent efforts of John Jympson and his team, splicing extracts from hundreds of feet of footage, provide a visual energy equivalent to the music being played.

Here again, speed was the watchword: with filming completed in seven weeks, there remained three and a half weeks to edit the film, secure the music track, add the dubbing and make the prints for cinema release. On top of this, with the daily increase in Beatlemania stimulating stories in the press of shooting mayhem, imminent break-up, illness, even haircuts, United Artists' executives were beginning to take more interest in their film project. In *Hollywood UK* Richard Lester congratulated his employers as 'the only company I knew who would say about a proposed project "We'll let you know by Friday" and then if they gave you the go ahead not see you again until the première'.[53] After a working preview, however, they contacted Shenson with instructions to wipe the Beatles' voices from the soundtrack and redub them with the more accessible tones of transatlantic professional actors. For Alexander Walker this is where Shenson's production is important: 'A less resolute producer, whose confidence in local accents hadn't been boosted by a fortune at the international box-office, might have yielded to pressure to give the film an American slant.'[54]

United Artists, though, were not going to make a fight over cinematic style or discourse. For all the effort being expended on the film by cast and crew, it was still viewed by company executives as largely an adjunct to what had suddenly become a surefire lucrative record deal. United Artists had insouciantly agreed to Jacobs's renegotiation of payment for the film, but central to the deal was a clause giving them the right to release the soundtrack on their own record label. When Epstein had relayed this news to EMI, it placed them in a difficult situation. EMI possessed an exclusive recording deal with the Beatles, but they were wary of upsetting the group or their manager (who was also responsible for a host of other EMI artists) if they were to jeopardise the film deal by insisting on keeping the recording rights. Eventually L. C. Wood, the managing director of EMI, skilfully negotiated a deal which gave United Artists the soundtrack album for North America (with a pressing fee to EMI) while EMI kept the rights for the rest of the world. He also got the film company to agree to allow Capitol to release the Beatles' tracks from the film, providing the album was not called *A Hard Day's Night*. The five new tracks were issued on *Something New* one month after the soundtrack was released. (EMI eventually got their hands on everything connected with the film when they bought United Artists Records in 1979.)

The Beatles' success in Britain had been swift but staggered: in America it was instant and total, and it is with the film soundtrack that the full force of Beatlemania in the United States can best be illustrated. United Artists had initially programmed 500,000 pressings of the album: they were hopeful of securing RIAA gold disc status but, in truth, with no precedent for the phenomenon sweeping the country, it was impossible to estimate demand with any degree of certainty. New York radio station WMCA then previewed the soundtrack on 25 June, however, a full ten days ahead of the official release, creating a nationwide response from record stores, eager to meet unending customer demand. This culminated in advance orders of over 2 million for the soundtrack album, making *A Hard Day's Night* potentially the biggest-selling album to date in the USA. Before the final print of the film had been released by the laboratory, the tie-in soundtrack album, itself still at the presses, had not only guaranteed itself number 1 position in the charts, but had ensured that the budget of £200,000 had already been exceeded twice over in profits.

This hysteria for the LP fed back into film demand, with America alone demanding a thousand prints. Britain had asked for 110, while worldwide an unprecedented order of between 1,500 and 1,800 prints were made. While the film was still in its frantic post-production phase, United Artists informed the media that, during August and September of 1964, *A Hard Day's Night* would be shown on a saturation basis in every available market around the world, with 'more prints in circulation than for any other pic in history'.[55]

In Britain, the film, replacing *Tom Jones*, was given a Royal World Première at the London Pavilion before HRH Princess Margaret and the Earl of Snowdon to aid the Dockland Settlements and the Variety Club Heart Fund on Monday, 6 July 1964. VIP seats were fifteen guineas each. Piccadilly Circus had to be closed to traffic as there were an estimated 20,000 fans crowding the area. Over two hundred policemen tried to keep order, while ambulance crews tended to over one hundred fans who fainted. The Northern première took place in Liverpool on 10 July at the Odeon Cinema, following a civic reception at the town hall. This was a tense affair, since the group had been accused of deserting their 'roots' when their success lead them to relocate to London. They were unsure of the reception their home fans would give them, but that trepidation soon turned to delight as over 150,000 people lined the ten-mile route from Speke – now renamed John Lennon – Airport to the city centre. On 2 August the film then went on general release in Britain and the rest of Europe. In Germany the film was known as *Yeah Yeah Yeah die Beatles*, in France as *Quatre Garçons dans le Vent*. In Italy, ironically, it was given the title of a Cliff Richard song from *The Young Ones*: *Tutti Per Uno* ('All for One').

In America, *A Hard Day's Night* was officially premièred at the Beacon Theatre in New York on 12 August and opened in 500 cinemas throughout the country the next day. Before then, however, United Artists revealed that over one hundred cities had requested an early print. These special previews and premières had brought in over half a million dollars. Such had been the demand for product associated with the Beatles that *A Hard Day's Night* had become the first film in the history of the motion picture industry to ensure a profit while filming was still in progress.

OH, IT'S A PLOT

The basic story of the film, as outlined in a press-pack synopsis by United Artists, is as follows:

Once upon a time there were four happy Liverpool lads called Paul, John, George and Ringo and they played their music all over the country. Now, when they'd finished playing in one place they'd run to the nearest railway station and go on to a new place and play some more of their music, usually pursued by hundreds of young ladies.

On the day of our story [to the accompaniment of 'A Hard Day's Night'], John, George and Ringo get to the station and fight their way into the railway compartment where they meet up with Paul, who has a little old man with him, a very dear little old man. Anyway, who is he? The little old man is 'Mixing' John McCartney, Paul's grandfather. Grandfather is dedicated to the principle of divide and conquer. The mere sight of a nice friendly group of clean-cut lads like the Beatles brings him out in a rash of counterplots.

Norm, the boys' road manager, who is conducting a war of nerves with John, the group's happy anarchist, collects Grandfather and together with Shake, the general dogsbody, he retreats to the restaurant car for coffee, leaving the boys to settle in for their journey to London and a live television show. However, a well-established first-class ticket holder drives the boys out of their carriage by being pompously officious, so they go and join Norm, Shake and Grandfather in the restaurant car.

By this time Grandfather has managed to get Norm and Shake at each other's throats and Paul warns the others that this could be only the beginning. Sure enough, Grandfather has started a campaign of dissension that leads to frightening schoolgirls, a proposal of marriage to a chance acquaintance and general chaos culminating with Grandfather being locked in the luggage van where he and the boys complete their journey making music [singing 'I Should Have Known Better'].

When the boys arrive in London, they go to their hotel, where Norm leaves them to sort out their fan mail. However, Grandfather has noticed that a certain amount of good-humoured banter is directed at Ringo. Here, thinks Grandfather, is the weak link in the chain. Instead of staying in the hotel the four boys sneak out to enjoy themselves at a twist club and Grandfather, trading his clothes for a waiter's suit, heads straight for a gambling club, passing himself off as Lord John McCartney. Again the boys have to rescue him, much to the old man's indignation.

The following day sees the boys plunged into the bustle of the television world. Press conferences, rehearsals [they perform 'If I Fell'], make-up, running from place to place, being shepherded by the harassed Norm and got at by the television show's neurotic director, and always in the background is Grandfather, interfering, disrupting and needling Ringo.

Only for a moment are the boys free. [As 'Can't Buy Me Love' plays] they can enjoy themselves playing in a large, open field, but even that doesn't last. John, however, does make the most of every second; he is always for the here and now. Paul tries keeping things on an even keel and George has a blind doggedness that sees him through. But the strain begins to tell on Ringo.

Grandfather, of course, plays on this, pointing out the barrenness of Ringo's life [after further rehearsals of 'And I Love Her' and 'I'm Happy Just to Dance with You'] and finally goading him into walking out into the world, outside of the group [Ringo's theme – 'This Boy'].

The other three boys go out searching for Ringo, leaving Norm to fume and the director to worry himself to near collapse at the possibility of no show.

Meanwhile, Ringo has found the world outside not too friendly, and through a series of encounters and misunderstandings, gets himself arrested. He is taken to the station, where he meets up with Grandfather, who has been taken into protective custody. Grandfather storms at the police sergeant and manages to escape, leaving Ringo behind in the police station.

He gets back to the television theatre and tells the boys, who, pursued again, but this time by the police, go and rescue Ringo ['Can't Buy Me Love' reprise].

Finally they are able to do their show in front of a live audience ['Tell Me Why', 'If I Fell', 'I Should Have Known Better' and 'She Loves You'].

The show does well, but as soon as it is finished, again it is the mad dash on to the next plane for the next show. The past thirty-six hours have been a hard day's night. The next thirty-six hours will he the same ['A Hard Day's Night' reprise].

TWO
Analysis

1. REVOLT ... ?

I'M A MOCKER!

The opening chord of 'A Hard Day's Night' – a G7 with added ninth and suspended fourth – has, for Ian MacDonald, 'a significance in Beatles lore matched only by the concluding E major of "A Day in the Life", the two opening and closing the group's middle period of peak creativity'.[1] It also signals the true opening of a new, middle phase in the British pop musical, a 'mature' phase that will problematise the status of pop fame and the media images that promote it. As part of those media this film knows that it contributes to the mythologising of its stars but simultaneously subjects that process to a distanced, critical analysis. It is a doubleness, a resistance to closure, that permeates every aspect of *A Hard Day's Night*, even its paradoxical title, and that prompts an active and collaborative engagement with a teasing, ironic complicity. Lyrically, songs such as 'Can't Buy Me Love' will deal with highly duplicitous forms of exchange, echoing those between stars, spectator and film, while visually, Lester's knowing use of quotation and connotation, of clichés in verbal and photographic form, further contribute to an ironic questioning of any literal understanding of realism. From the outset the *cinéma-vérité* style is thrown into doubt: above all there is the duality inherent in the filming of the public space. For instance, seconds into the film George clearly takes a genuine tumble as crowds of fans and photographers add to the confusion of what was supposed to be an entirely staged chase. Are the Beatles filming or really fleeing their ubiquitous aficionados, or does such a division become meaningless in the context of their effect on young extras?

As the train pulls out of Paddington Station, with it go the last vestiges of the 'primitive', coffee bar and Cliff pop musical. As soon as they are settled in their carriage we are privy to the wisecracking quartet, teasing rather than respecting their elders. The target of this impudence is initially Paul's grandfather, whom the Beatles constantly refer to as 'clean'. The motiveless repetition of this epithet makes us quickly realise that we are not going to get a full understanding of the boys: some jokes seem for their ears only. Is he a 'clean' as opposed to a 'dirty' old man (Harold's habitual description of his father, Albert Steptoe)? Maybe, though the part had been written before the casting of Brambell – Dermot Kelly had been first choice. Perhaps the group are mocking their own Epstein-inspired image: one could tentatively point to the fact that the word was musical anathema to John Lennon, who told Billy J. Kramer that it was his great ambition 'to blow the Shadows out – he couldn't stand their clean music'.[2]

While the adjective floats in the air, 'Mixing' John McCartney is immediately taken off for a coffee and his place in the carriage is taken by a bowler-hatted first-class ticket holder who asserts his authority by closing the window and turning off Ringo's radio. Here is an unmistakable figure of the establishment, the older, parental generation. He is impolite and unfriendly, unlike the Fab Four: he is the one to swear, referring to their radio as 'that damn thing!' The Beatles try to articulate the rights of young people in a democratic society – four out of five want the window open – but to no avail. He answers with 'I fought the war for your sort', to which Ringo replies 'Bet you're sorry you won'. John flutters his eyelids and asks the man to 'give us a kiss': he fumes and returns to his newspaper. As the man is impervious to reasoning, the Beatles resort to humour, exaggerating the role he has consigned them to, troublesome schoolboys who want their ball back. It is a further switch in mood: until now the film we have been watching has adhered to the tenets of realism, but suddenly the group appear outside the carriage window as the train is in motion. Also, where the traditional pop musical would finish in mutual understanding, here the Beatles walk out, leaving the city gent to his prejudices. This film, like its heroes, will not obey the rules.

This exchange is an early foregrounding of a new phenomenon: the irreverence of the young, their spirit of rebellion. Exciting for some, this aspect dampened enthusiasm for others. Ann Scott-Jones wrote that: 'The thing about the Beatles' film which nobody has mentioned is its total remorselessness. This is a comedy without one twinge of pity for human beings, particularly the old. *A Hard Day's Night* is brilliant, fast, funny and distinctly frightening. I had thought of the Beatles as witty, talented, charming boys, but they are also as hard as old iron.'[3] The critic of the right-wing *Daily Mail* could have taken this further, since the man in the carriage represents not just declining age but moribund class. He clearly feels that the Beatles, in spite of their sartorial neatness, are socially inferior and so instructs them to take their radio 'into the corridor or some other part of the train where you so obviously belong!' It was an early signposting from Richard Lester, the 'outsider looking in', who had been struck by the group's attitude to social barriers:

> The general aim of the film was to present what was apparently becoming a social phenomenon in this country. Anarchy is too strong a word, but the quality of confidence that the boys exuded ... You must accept that this is a film based on a class society. It is difficult for someone coming from America, where there is a society based on money, to realise the strength ... I mean a society that was still based on privilege – privilege by schooling, privilege by birth, privilege by accent, privilege by speech. They were the first people to attack this ... they said if you want to do something, do it. You can do it. Forget all this talk about talent or ability or money or speech. Just do it. And this has been their great strength.[4]

A problem with Lester's reading is that while the film emphasises the group's own working-class roots it needs a broad definition of 'working-class' to include any of the quartet other than Ringo. Second, however one defines their social origins, the Beatles' education and wealth meant they were now leaving those environs faster than a speeding train. Nevertheless, this persona-creating film makes several references to them being ordinary, working-class lads – and not yet ironically, as at the start of *Help!*. Much of this centres on the anthropological staple of food. For example, there is George's attachment to home-made sandwiches: he is seen eating them on the train at the start of the film, and during the press conference as a journalist stuffs a cream cake in his mouth we hear George saying 'and me mother asked before we left for America if I wanted any sandwiches'. After fleeing the freeloading journalists, John complains that he 'didn't even get a jam butty'. When Ringo escapes to a London pub, far from Norm's prediction of wine, women and song, he buys himself a stale sandwich, a pint of bitter and has a game of darts. Paul shows his working-class worth not just by caring for his 'heartbroken' but distinctly proletarian grandfather (the baggage of Brambell's role as Steptoe Senior reinforcing this class placement for the fictional family addition), but also, emphatically yet knowingly, by pronouncing the final 't' when he reads out Ringo's invitation to a 'champagne buffet'.

However duplicitous the reality, class, at least for British audiences, was a key ingredient in the attraction of the Beatles. Here, as Richard Buskin notes, were 'four ordinary boys next door ... living out a fantasy on behalf of everyone else'.[5] To this can be added nationality, as the group's global success made them patriotic symbols of a new social mobility and the 'classlessness' that was advocated as the way ahead for 1960s Britain. This was also largely a matter of geographical acceptance, and Alun Owen's script skilfully exploits the Beatles' provincial appeal, adding a number of slang phrases to their dialogue that made no concessions to London, let alone Los Angeles. Things are 'gear' or 'grotty' – a word asked after by Princess Margaret at the première and which entered the national consciousness and the OED after Owen's screenplay.

It would be wrong, though, to categorise this as cognate to the new social realism, recording an emergent meritocracy as in *Room at the Top* (1959) or even *This Sporting Life* (1963). Wherever we place the Beatles in Britain's class structure, they are the antithesis of the downtrodden working men and women that Jack Clayton, Lindsay Anderson, John Schlesinger and Tony Richardson had depicted. Instead this film shows their ability to project what Simon Frith has called 'a politics of optimism'.[6] The boys are upbeat and exuberant, moving, by necessity, in an arts-and-media middle-class environment (contrasting with *Expresso Bongo*, where Johnny Jackson is not a success and has to survive in a poor and seedy, insecure environment). For Charlie Gillett the social realist authors and film-makers 'had social messages to get across, and the characters inevitably came second, functioning as conduits for the writers' ideologies'. The Beatles, though, 'exploded this image of working-class youth'. For Gillett, 'their social message was rarely expressed, but hung about their heads like an aura of impatience with convention and evident satisfaction with wealth and fame'.[7] This fame has obvious advantages: not only access to most of the young women they encounter – the schoolgirls on the train are happy to follow the boys to the luggage van and they have plenty of female company in the nightclub – but also entry to any venue they care to visit. As they arrive at the casino in pursuit of McCartney Senior, a doorman blocks their entry. Officious doormen proved a persistent obstacle to Craig Douglas and Helen Shapiro in *It's Trad Dad!*, but here, Norm only has to nod towards the Beatles and the doorman steps aside, smiling in recognition. All doors – and all classes – are now open to the Beatles and their filmed life.

Using this open access, *A Hard Day's Night* investigates how a commercially-oriented 'artistic' generation – the middle-class media professional – tries to capitalise on and break in this latest craze; as such the film explores its own ostensible purpose – exploitation. In the hastily constructed press conference sequence, the media's tendency literally to feed off the fame of the Beatles is strongly signalled. The press party had been a staple ingredient of the British pop musical, framing *The Tommy Steele Story*, ending *Summer Holiday*, undercutting Dixie Collins in *Expresso Bongo*. While the boys cannot get hold of any food and drink at this reception supposedly held in their honour, the press gorge themselves so busily that they do not even notice the Beatles leaving. The sequence is most fondly remembered for the quick-witted responses of the Beatles, a display of verbal skill and a gift for the satirical put-down that caused so many critics of the time to think of the Marx Brothers. More importantly, though, it represents a confrontation between the values of the 1950s and those of the 1960s. Where Tommy Steele would sit quietly and reply politely to the condescending questions of the middle-class press, the Beatles answer back. The different social class of the press from that of the Beatles is evident from their accents, their patronising manner, their fashion sense – two women in flowery hats seem straight from Steele at the Café de Paris – and their consequent obsession with the Beatles' own appearance. Faced with the Fab Four (and many, remember, were real journalists roped in for the sequence), they constitute a class and a mind frame that seem suddenly to be way off the pace. As the Beatles run verbal rings round the writers, they proclaim a social victory as well. And yet all is done in such good taste. The Beatles mock the predictability of the parasitic press but, in spite of the strains placed on them by their own celebrity, they remain generally friendly towards others, unaltered by their constant presence in the spotlight.

Their attitude differs in degree but in not in kind towards the highly-strung and short-tempered television director (Victor Spinetti) who, after the train commuter, becomes the main target for the Beatles' antiphonal stance towards authority. Having fretted over the group's whereabouts, he is finally greeted by John's sarcastic 'Standing around, eh? Some people have it dead easy!' The director, for once powerless to direct, complains that 'Once you're over thirty, you're past it. It's a young man's game!' It seems here that the Beatles, aware of their cultural capital, perform entirely on their own terms: while the director can only stamp his feet and make vague threats that 'there'll be trouble', the Beatles manifestly have the power to trouble his career – their appearance is a bigger coup for him than for them. When they finally deign to appear, the director is overcome with gratitude, since he faced the ultimate sanction, expulsion from the media capital and the vibrancy of pop: 'If you hadn't returned it would have meant *The Epilogue*, or *News in Welsh* – for life!' His frenzied relief stands in sharp contrast to the calm and collected Fab Four. Throughout they show themselves more competent and self-assured than the older generation in the industry: their parading and their pranks never seriously jeopardise their crowd-pleasing professionalism and by focusing on the Beatles' engaging approach to both work and play *A Hard Day's Night* registers a collapsing together of the primitive pop musical's distinctions between 'youth-as-fun' and 'youth-as-trouble'. They accede to the director's timetable, they refrain from admonishing Paul's grandfather: rather than being as hard as old iron the boys are established as essentially soft-centred.

A Hard Day's Night knows itself to be a commodification of the Fab Four, but the film is not afraid to attack that cynically programmed process. In a scene that makes an astute critique of this merchandising of youth, Kenneth Haigh (keen to keep a distance as an actor) appears as professional style-guru Simon Marshall, looking to identify and exploit the teenage market. George is mistaken for their latest male model: when introduced to Simon the latter enthuses – 'Not really bad. Turn around, baby. Oh yes, he's a definite poss.' His ignorance of who George 'really' is emphasises his incompetence and like the TV director he lacks the boys' mental equilibrium, their politeness, their 'common' decency. When the Beatle tries to explain Simon assumes the accent is just for effect: 'Oh you can come off it with us. You don't have to do all the old adenoidal glottal stop and carry-on for our benefit.' He is initially disconcerted when he realises that George is 'a natural': he tells his secretary that 'you know by now that phoneys are much easier to handle' – a self-reflective comment on the preference of the media (and hence *A Hard Day's Night*) for image over reality. George's job would be to give his opinion on some clothes for teenagers – 'not your real opinion, naturally. It'll be written out and you'll learn it.' Here is more, though minor, self-reflection: in what seems like a jibe from the classical actor to the novice, an in-joke at Owen's staccato script, Simon asks George if he can 'read'. 'I mean lines, ducky. Can you handle lines?' The amateur copes admirably.

Throughout the style-guru reveals a patronising parasitism: while earning a good living from teenage fashion, Simon does nothing to conceal his contempt for the teenagers and their culture: 'Give him whatever it is they drink: Cocarama?' he instructs his assistant. When George is given the shirts to look at Simon informs him that 'You'll like these. You'll really "dig" them. They're "fab" and all those other pimply hyperbole.' Here the film foregrounds the argot of rebellion. Unsure of the discourse of the youth he aims to influence, Simon is bewildered when George dismisses their new range of shirts as 'dead grotty', but asks that the word be noted for Susan, the agency's 'real trend-setter'. This exchange encapsulates a perfect paradigm of the life cycle for 'trendy' language: a word, originating on the street, is incorporated into celebrity discourse, before perishing on the calculating lips of advertising. Simon is then horrified when Harrison rejects their resident teenage icon 'Susan' as 'a drag, a well-known drag'. In a move that shows the perceived transience of the new fashions, Simon checks his calendar. No, there are at least three weeks left before trends change and so George and his 'utterly valueless opinions' are sent packing: 'The new thing,' Simon retorts, 'is to care passionately and to be right-wing.' Harold Wilson's triumphant entry proves the style-guru's error of judgement in the political sphere; George's casual exit ('I don't care!') shows him wrong on the current personal stance. More than this, though, the whole scene serves to show that George, like the other Beatles, is 'real', 'a natural', and not a mere marketed product. Which is, of course, both true and not true.

FRATERNISING WITH PRISONERS

In spite of their youthful self-assurance and social mobility not all is sweetness and light for the Fab Four. In another aspect of the film's doubleness, the boys are shown to have the whole world at their feet yet cannot leave their front door and walk on the street in safety. This is clear from the opening shots of *A Hard Day's Night*, which illustrate that this film will explore the phenomenon then sweeping the media: Beatlemania. Armed with privileged access behind the scenes, it proceeds to investigate the response to this unprecedented cultural happening of the caught-unawares media machine and to record the nature of the fan base feeding into this mass hysteria. Above all, though, this 'process' movie allows us to see how Beatlemania affects the boys themselves – and for the most part this is not seen as a pleasurable existence. Caveats must, of course, be entered. In the 'real' chauffeur-driven escape, John and Paul bask in their adulation; Paul laughs as the admiring make-up girls are hurried off stage; John is especially amused

4. *'If I Fell'. Immediate claustrophobia.*

when George takes his early fall; when Millie concludes their face-off by stating that 'you don't look like him at all' John goes off in a huff, slighted because his famed features have not been recognised.

Overall, though, as George Melly noted, 'they were victims not victors. They were as trapped as any working-class boy or girl in a dead-end job.'[8] The opening frames of *A Hard Day's Night* show three of the Beatles running for cover from hysterical fans, hemmed in screen left between the harsh verticals of a large brick wall with drainpipes and a central row of lamp-posts, while parked cars and 'real' fans fill the right side of the frame. This is not to be a rags-to-riches bio-pic as in *The Tommy Steele Story*: here from the outset running straight towards and then past us as their pursuers fill the screen are recognisable celebrities, enduring at least as much as enjoying the trappings of stardom. Fame brings not freedom to do as one likes but the claustrophobia and paranoia observed by Shenson at his first meeting with the group. This sense of constant incarceration had been the major reaction of all those involved with creating the group's debut film vehicle, as Alun Owen explained to Alexander Walker: 'Ever noticed how much celebrities are pushed around in public? Really pushed around? Managers guiding them, fans pulling at them, compères patting them. You get to feel so much moveable property. What it feels like to be a Beatle: that's the first priority.'[9] The film's opening ensures that this sense of incarceration is also the spectator's initial perception.

The train itself is a vehicle less of escape than a reduced oppression:

as it leaves the platform, the shot from inside the Beatles' compartment is of hoards of screaming fans and the click, click, click of camera flashes. Their status is highlighted by Grandfather, who thwarts the boys' advances to two schoolgirls by warning them not to 'fraternise with my prisoners. Convicts in transit ... Typical old lags, the lot of them.' The allusion is not lost on John, who plays up to the role when they again meet the girls: 'We've broken out; oh the blessed freedom of it all!' He extends his hands and pleads, 'Have you got a nail file – these handcuffs are killing me' before adding a cinematic layer to his unwarranted captivity: 'I was framed.' When the group perform their first song, 'I Should Have Known Better', they are framed cage-like in the luggage compartment, the girls close around them. When they reach their hotel room, they are still prisoners of their celebrity, forced to stay in and answer their fan mail. The theme remains a constant stylistically, verbally and structurally. Scenes are habitually shot in small rooms and dark corridors. Norm resembles a jailer, returning them to their dressing room after the first rehearsal with the threat to keep them there 'even if I have to put the key in the lock and turn it'. Later, after another escape, he confides wryly that he had 'considered a ball and chain'. Finally, just prior to their concert, the group are chased around London by the police, a parallel to the film's opening sequence.

Lester recalled John's comment after his visit to Sweden about cars and rooms and rooms and cars: 'So that feeling of claustrophobia was how we tried to think of the whole first sequence, the whole first third of the film. In closed spaces: prisoners in space, prisoners of fans, prisoners by car, train, small hotel rooms – do this, do that, sign this.'[10] Tactfully, though, John's real-life complaint about the trip to Sweden is here placed, almost word for word, into the mouth of Paul's fictional grandfather (the only character eventually handcuffed) who moans that 'I thought I was getting a change of scenery and so far I've been in a train and a room and a car and a room and a room and a room ... I'm feeling decidedly straitjacketed!' The displacement of this comment to Paul's grandfather was astute, since to attribute it to John, or any Beatle, would have conveyed a sense of peevish ingratitude. Instead the older generation's brief exposure to the group's daily experience allows the viewer to sympathise by proxy.

Lester termed the Beatles 'revolutionaries in a goldfish bowl',[11] and an auteurist reading of his work would point to the recurrence of this theme: the lot of the idolised hero. Flashman in *Royal Flash* (1975), Robin Hood in *Robin and Marian* (1976), Superman in *Superman 2*

(1981) are all heroic figures subjected to a degree of fan worship that precludes the ability to live a normal life. But does this new-found social mobility and Scouse mockery really provide the Beatles with the status of rock revolutionaries? Does the group laugh out of credence anyone or anything smacking of authority? Is the truth not that, for all their cheeky opposition to such forces, in train compartment, in studio, in press conference, in dealings with the police, the Beatles fail to constitute any real challenge or resistance? Paul quotes 'up the workers ... and all that stuff', but it carries no conviction: it is a trendy catchphrase, meaning no more politically than his Mao-style collarless jacket. John Lennon comments on 'the older generation leading this country to galloping ruin' but as he does so removes the sting from the barb by admiring himself in the mirror in his false black beard. If one looks for radical protest, one must always place it in the comic register, and 'secure fun' is a double-edged sword when the Beatles' targets are reduced to caricatured buffoons or Keystone Kops. The clowning of the Marx Brothers had, as Howard Jacobson notes, 'a ferocious, demoniacal quality'. It was not 'sheer anarchic craziness', but 'violent and vengefully destructive, performed as though by brilliant imps of malevolence, damaging because damaged'.[12] The Beatles, by comparison, are joyously antic, pop pranksters who will show up the pompous, the pedestrian and the pretentious, but who take their cue from Milligan before the Marxes, Karl or Groucho.

And while George Melly sees Elvis Presley as the apex of the emasculation of rock'n'roll, one must hesitate before claiming that the Beatles are either immune to or are embodiments of this movement from revolt into style. For as with Tommy Steele and Cliff Richard there seems little evidence of any concerted desire to 'revolt'. Dave Harker points out how readily 'these happy little rockers accepted the uniforms, submitted to stylised versions of long hair, made sweeter music and became an even bigger commercial success. They became, in short, thoroughly respectable.'[13] What do the Beatles do that could be construed as radical? They might be difficult to control, but this is playful, mischief – more like 'Mister, can I have my ball back?' than they might care to admit. Throughout, humour and the conventions of the musical genre nullify any offence in the areas of youthful independence, class conflict and sexual promiscuity. As much as Cliff, they remain the nice boy next door whose records you could buy with impunity.

If one is looking for malevolence and violence, then one needs to look either side of the boys' pivotal position. In truth, the harder-hitting social critiques come from McCartney Senior. His presence is often considered the weakest area of the plot, but as 'a soldier of the Republic' he allows an outsider's angle on the class and legal system. Grandfather McCartney knows just as well as his grandson how to play a game of appearance: taking a waiter's formal dress to pass as one of the elite at an exclusive gambling casino, his actions expose an acceptance of dress redolent of Buñuel's depiction of the charm of the bourgeoisie. Though he plays chemmy with cries of 'Soufflé!' instead of 'Suivez' and 'Bingo!' instead of 'Banco', the suit alone enables Paul's plebeian grandfather to convince the casino manager that he is Lord John McCartney, 'Irish peer, filthy rich'. To emphasise the mere veneer, the façade of privilege, when he runs out of tokens to play at the table, 'Mixer' McCartney merely places a towel over his forearm and lowers his head obsequiously to metamorphose into a waiter so as to collect money from a gullible customer. The legally aware Irishness comes across strongly when in the police station: here, instead of the Beatles' silent-movie chase through the streets, the nature of the grandfather's abuse to the police pushes at the edges of caricature, coming close to genuine subversion. 'I know your game. You'll get me into the charge room and out'll come the rubber hoses.' He enumerates their punishments: 'the kidney punch and the rabbit clout, the third degree and the size-twelve-boot ankle tap'. He then declares his Republican allegiance, starting to sing 'A Nation Once Again'. Lester later admitted that Brambell's strong Irish accent 'somehow allowed an uncalculated aggressiveness to emerge that was different from the passive cunning of Steptoe Senior'.[14] It is not the Beatles but the ex-scrap-and-bone man who is as hard as any old iron.

PUT THEM GIRLS DOWN!

The one area of *A Hard Day's Night* where the Beatles' behaviour is more overtly opposed to respectability is in its approach to sex. Hanif Kureishi suggests that 'Pop was made for the moment, to embody exhilaration, and it sprang from a momentary but powerful impulse: teenage sexual longing.'[15] Such sexuality as was visible in pop films (censorship in the early 1960s was particularly protective and proscriptive towards the young) was essentially heterosexual and channelled through the male white star of the film. And that sexuality, until the Beatles hit the screen, had always been implied, but never indulged. In *Serious Charge*, Cliff Richard's brother might post-coitally tuck his shirt into his jeans and in *Beat Girl* Adam Faith's Bardot-cloned friend might begin a striptease in her living room, but the stars themselves remained chaste and chaseable. Sexuality had bubbled just below the surface of most pop musical films up to 1964: with *A Hard Day's Night*, as seen in the climactic concert performance, it burst out.

In a film constructed so essentially around the Beatles, it would be difficult to find evidence of anything other than white male heterosexuality in *A Hard Day's Night*. While only John and Paul are depicted as being constantly 'on the pull', the film ensures that each member of the Beatles is shown to be interested in girls. When walking along in disguise, Ringo doubles back to chat up a young girl and George looks on approvingly at the legs of the secretary in the style studio. In one scene, all four lure their individual make-up artiste away from their duties in the depths of the green room. It begins when John tells his obliging blonde assistant, 'I can get you on the stage.' On being asked how, he replies, 'Turn right in the corridor and go past ... ' Although the scene is played as a joke, it undermines the traditional boy–girl, star–crew member binary purpose of the musical: John's proposal clearly has nothing to do with marriage. It becomes more risqué when the immediate context is understood: Brown and Gaines point out that during filming 'the young girls on the set being used as extras were discreetly lured into the [Beatles'] trailers for quickies between takes'.[16] A knowledge of the Maysles Brothers' contemporary documentary reinforces a wider view of opportunity knocking, and young girls being knocked off.

The confident, successful sexuality of the Beatles, sometimes governed by self-restraint, more often thwarted by the actions of others (including Richard Lester who, according to Victor Spinetti, left many of their more explicit ad-libs on the cutting-room floor)[17] is enhanced by the comparative physical unattractiveness of those around them. No other young men appear: Norm and Shake take no obvious interest in the opposite sex, even when they follow the boys to the nightclub; the middle-aged men encountered at the television studios (Spinetti, Haigh and Robin Ray) are all played as camp and, worse still, have distinctly middle-class accents. Class here is again significant for, as Susan Hayward points out, racial and class differences are categories that gender ideology seeks to dissimulate: 'Why otherwise the prurience with the potency of the Black male or the working-class hero? They are perceived first as their sex and sexuality.'[18] It all becomes a question of context: whatever our categorisation of social origins, in the effete, bourgeois environment of the media, each Beatle is, as John would later sing, 'a working-class hero' and the potency lies with the pop star proletariat.

Paul's grandfather is the only other character who is able to attract the opposite sex, though his advances – turning to a well-endowed woman leaning over his shoulder at the casino and saying 'I bet you're a good swimmer!' – are redolent mostly of Donald McGill and times long gone. When he asks Ringo, 'When was the last time you gave a girl a pink-edged daisy? When did you last embarrass a Sheila with your cool appraising stare?', Ringo replies severely: 'You're a bit old for that sort of chat, aren't you?' The open display of sexuality is permitted only to the young and – *pace* Ringo – the handsome.

In the concert scene the camera moves rapidly between the faces of the Beatles and their audience. Close-ups of the latter show girls in tears, in ecstasy, but clearly mouthing the name of their favourite Beatle. It may seem excessive to describe this intensity of emotions as orgasmic, but in his interview with the Beatles in 1964 Michael Braun mentions that 'John said that they have been told that girls masturbate when they are on the stage'.[19] (Aware his lyrics could not be heard, John was also prone to sing 'I Want to Hold Your Gland'.) Clearly the relationship between audience and performers relies (almost) entirely on the developing heterosexuality of the former and the confirmed heterosexuality of the latter for its very existence.

'Almost', because the above does not mean that there are no overtones of homosexuality in the film. Musically and narratively, these focus on John. Yes, Paul's composition 'Can't Buy Me Love', which accompanies the boys' cavorting in a field and running through the streets with policemen in hot pursuit, is not directed to 'my love' or 'my dear' but to the more sexually ambiguous 'my friend'. But more pointedly, more personally, when John sings the love song 'If I Fell' during a studio rehearsal, it is not to a girl but to Ringo. When arguing with the commuter on the train, John flutters his eyelashes at him and says 'Give us a kiss!' On passing an actor in Regency dress and powdered wig, he exclaims 'Gear costume', the actor eyes him up and down before replying 'Swap', to which John answers with a suggestive 'Cheeky!' In the make-up room, though sporting a fake beard, John introduces himself as 'Betty'. When Paul sees a young blonde assistant following the show's producer to the control room, he says, 'I bet his wife doesn't know about her!' John, however, seems more aware of his sexual persuasion: 'I bet he hasn't even got a wife; look at his sweater!'

Elsewhere references are more implicit – coded even – but still centred on John. When in the make-up room, John notices Ringo's magazine and cries out excitedly: 'Hey, he's reading *The Queen*.' Turning round almost straight to camera he adds: 'That's an in joke, you know.' Paul's grandfather immediately gives his 'considered opinion that you're all a bunch of sissies'. 'You're just jealous,' John replies before Norm intercedes: 'Now leave them alone or I'll tell them the truth about you, Lennon.' The threat both indicates the fictitious nature of the film being acted out, and implies revelations of a sexual nature, the very voicing of which points to a more sexually secure 'real' Beatle, for John Lennon enjoyed an ambivalent relationship with his real-life manager, Brian Epstein. John knew that Brian was attracted to him, yet the two took a twelve-day break together in Barcelona at the end of April 1963, a trip which occasioned rumours as to what might (or might not) have happened there – and formed the starting point for a superior Beatles' bio-pic, Christopher Munch's *The Hours and Times* (1992). On his return John took exception to the innuendos and one drunken night beat up compère Bob Wooler. The brawl made the *Daily Mirror*, but the cause of the spat was not divulged. John was contrite for his actions: later Tom Robinson would claim that Lennon wrote the first gay rock song, with 'You've Got to Hide Your Love Away' in 1965 being addressed to Brian Epstein.[20] Back in early 1964 though, John could be seen as more able to laugh off any aspersions as to his sexuality: Norm's comment can thus be read as a continuation of the 'in joke'.

It must be emphasised, however, that all these references, candid or cryptic, are humorous and therefore remain at the level of undertone; the film cannot allow anything other than the heterosexual nature of its male lead performers to be displayed. As Stephen Bourne notes, 'The Beatles may wear their hair long, but they're *real* men!'[21] For Bourne, 'the gay characters who exist in this film are objects of ridicule' who 'exist only for comic relief and, no doubt, to reaffirm the Fab Four's heterosexuality'.[22] First there is the crew at the television studios. Bourne describes Spinetti's character as 'a bossy, wrist-flapping television director. This obnoxious screaming queen is dressed in a fluffy sweater and orders his effeminate floor manager (Robin Ray) about the TV studio.'[23] When Ringo drops a drumstick, Ray picks it up and gently hits at the cymbals. Ringo shouts at him to stop. 'Oh surely I could just have a little touch,' Ray pleads with double meaning. Bourne also picks out Kenneth Haigh's Simon as 'the camp head of an advertising agency', who is 'helped by his gay assistant Adrian (Julian Holloway)'.[24]

Bourne concludes his study by speaking of 'the film's homophobia'.[25] However, alongside the girls chasing after the Beatles and screaming at their concerts, young men are also clearly visible. The concert is not just a final union of 'boy gets girl' and vice versa. In *The Beatles Anthology*, George Harrison spoke of noticing, during their stint in Paris in January 1964, 'slightly gay-looking boys at the stage door shouting "Ringo! Ringo!"'[26] It is open to, but not out of the question, that these young fans are gay, and one should emphasise that these boys are no more picked out for ridicule or relief than the screaming girls. The Beatles, after all, were publicly inclusive: they sought a total market penetration.

The inherent paternalistic ideology of the musical film is seen at an overt level in the Hollywood and early British pop musical: *A Hard Day's Night* unfolds a more ambivalent stance. Although co-operation between young and old is promoted, in the relationship between the Beatles and Paul's grandfather, and in the way the group eventually conform to the expectations of the television producer, the stereotypes of earlier pop musicals are not systematically employed. Bob Neaverson points out that Norm is presented, not as a conniving manager (such as the agent played by Laurence Harvey in *Expresso Bongo*), but 'as honest and practical (if a little bossy)' while 'Paul's trouble-stirring grandfather is depicted as something of a *senile* delinquent, a self-conscious reversal of traditional stereotyping'.[27] As Paul declares, it is not the young but his grandfather who 'hates group unity'. It is difficult to discover, however, whether a similar ambivalence also applies to gender roles since there are so few female characters to discuss. In the Presley films and the Cliff Richard trilogy, there was always a love interest between the lead male character and his 'steady' girlfriend, where inevitable misunderstandings were cleared up by the final song. Peter Brown and Steven Gaines maintain that, in the early days of the Beatles' success, Brian Epstein felt that 'publicly acknowledging any of the single Beatles' relationships with any one girl would be disastrous for the image'[28] and Walter Shenson et al. heeded advice to ensure the centrality of this stance to *A Hard Day's Night*. Yet this does not obviate references to the Beatles' predatory masculinity. They frequently attempt to initiate relationships with women, but their train and theatre chat-ups remain in the public domain, and all are frustrated by a figure of authority: Paul's grandfather, Norm, the senior make-up artist. On those occasions where the initiative is taken by a woman, then it is the individual Beatle who cuts short the liaison: when invited by a well-dressed woman into her compartment Ringo fears for his drumskins, while the surreal encounter between John and Millie on the theatre stairs is one of sexual allusion, mistaken identity and disconnected dialogue, John departing with the quip 'she's more like him than I am'. This rejection of female advances displays a typical male-gendered dominance in entering male–female relationships, but no relationship is allowed to progress: power lies in the hands of visible authority (in so far as relationships are concerned) or external authority (the Beatles and their entourage have no say in where they go or what they do). The typical male gender power role is present, but in a diluted form. There is a sense that the Beatles themselves are trying, without success, to break free from their carefully packaged personae. All, though, is played for humour, preventing the group from appearing too promiscuous, and the scenes that make the final edit maintain – just – their literally clean-cut image.

Which brings us back, finally, to the fans, the true believers. At the opening of the film, the first thing heard after the introduction song is the ululation of young female voices. Only two female characters have more than a single line to speak; Millie (perhaps a figure of minor authority backstage) speaks nonsense, the second speaks sensibly but is a secretary, a figure with no ostensible power or influence. It would seem that in *A Hard Day's Night* the female is rendered inarticulate or inaudible, or else she remains silent. She is, in essence, powerless. In terms of those appearing on screen, many more girls and women appear than boys or men, but at the level of plot the female is passive, the male active. It is a dynamic that takes one back to the title track, where Paul sings that 'when I'm home / Everything seems to be right. When I'm home / Feeling you holding me tight'. It is a patriarchal paradigm, the male singer's responsible labour rewarded at the end of the day by the care of his waiting woman.

Any survey of popular music must concede that its major players, from the exponents of the early skiffle boom through to the beat explosion of the 1960s were almost exclusively male: women's importance in popular music lay primarily in their position as energetic consumers. Female fanaticism was not unique to the post-war era – Rudolph Valentino elicited open devotion in the 1920s and 1930s – but in the late 1950s, this behaviour became more specifically associated with the relationship between teenage girls and pop musicians. The 'teenybopper', largely wiped from the filmed life of Tommy Steele, was given due time and attention in the Beatles' own 'day in the life'. Paul Johnson would infamously berate the group's fans for displaying 'a bottomless chasm of vacuity', girls with 'huge faces, bloated with cheap confectionery and smeared with chain-store make-up, the open, sagging mouths and glazed eyes' proving 'a collective portrait of a generation enslaved by a commercial machine'.[29] This is rightly considered a patronising and chauvinist description, yet later feminist critics also castigated practices that socialised young women into the subordinate gender role of 'adoring female in awe of the male on a pedestal'.[30] Yet Richard Lester is more assertive in his depiction, revealing (through first-hand experience on set) female fandom as a more active presence. *A Hard Day's Night* shows the fans chasing after the Beatles in its opening scenes, they scream out their desires at its end; their affective power as fans is present everywhere. The film reveals their potential to participate in displays of collective power, to overtake public spaces, to twist and shout a transgressive path beyond the bounds of genteel conformity. For potentially violent insurrection, it is not only to McCartney Senior but also to these young fans that we must turn our attention: the Beatles are just its pretext.

And yet. It can appear that another source of power available to the female is that of consumer, where she may dictate, through her purchasing power, the fate of her proffered idols. But this is problematic since *A Hard Day's Night* itself can be interpreted as an attempt to remove that power, to specify which of the products on the market she should support. From the very start of the film, hiding – significantly – in the photo-booth, through re-creations of famed Hoffmann images, on to its conclusion when Grandfather McCartney's forged photos rain down from the helicopter, we see the Beatles reproduced in still photographic form. It is a theme repeated throughout the film's staccato, cut-up, literally 'clichéd' style. For Jon Lewis, 'what we gain access to is a Beatles' (filmic) scrapbook, a collection of images that define our role as fans, as consumers of their stardom'.[31]

It is in many ways an act of faith. The film has reiterated how the reality of the Beatles escapes the medium: our consumption is only of a symbol, mass-produced at so many removes that only belief can confer authentification; as Catterall and Wells note, those final images scatter *faked* autographs 'by extension, into cinemagoers' laps everywhere'.[32] One specific example corroborates this: with John away at his Foyles' literary lunch, two of the dancing shoes seen during 'Can't Buy Me Love' belonged to Lester himself, gallantly stepping into the breach;

even the famous Beatle boots are fake. Nevertheless, those images of dancing feet and happy heads lying on the blanched ground are reminiscent of the more overtly sexual ecstasy portrayed in Fellini's *La Dolce Vita* (1960), an earlier attempt to film a new world in terms so urgent and ephemeral that it, like the Beatles' film, was termed 'a filmed newspaper'.[33] Unlike the closing frames of *It's Trad, Dad!* however, Lester's follow-up pop musical, for all its disposable imagery, presages a more lasting influence. *A Hard Day's Night*'s closing shot of the helicopter rising to the heavens is again redolent of Fellini's film, an echo of its opening where a giant statue of Christ the Redeemer is lifted by helicopter across the Roman skyline. Here Lester is subtly, intertextually showing what Lennon would stupidly, internationally tell: that the Beatles were replacing Jesus as the dominant icon of the airways, the purveyors of a new and secular Gospel of Happiness.

2. ... INTO STYLE

GROUP UNITY

More evident than any religious allusion, the BEA logo on·the helicopter door, incorporating the group in its corporate identity, reminds us that this film is, above all else, a means to sell Beatles product. Charlie Gillett notes that, on both sides of the Atlantic, 'the extent of the group's impact was more visual and social than musical' and depended on intensive media coverage.[34] However named, façade, style or image, as the scene between George and the professional trend-spotter underlines, was essential to this 'selling' and Brian Epstein's earliest strategy had been to repackage the group to make them acceptable to young and old alike. The most evident way this was achieved was in the Beatles' clothing. Before signing with Epstein the group wore rock'n'roll leather jackets and blue jeans – the look of Curley Thompson in *Serious Charge*. Conscious of the associations of such dress with juvenile delinquency – with sexual and violent excess – Epstein had persuaded the boys to wear the newly designed Beatle suit, the epitome of 'smart casual'. Nigel Whiteley, disagreeing slightly with David Harker, points out the duality denoted in their single-breasted jackets: 'the aim of the Beatle suit was to strike a balance between rebellion and respectability – rebelliousness to appeal to youth, respectability to soothe the parents – an aim that was successful'.[35] This success was not just rescuing the group from an image of youth-oriented aggression into one of universal acceptability, but was also a rejection of an American iconography for an indigenous sense of 'theatrical costume'. This is highlighted in the film's setting, which allows the Beatles several costume changes and make-up close-ups – situations that emphasise the Beatles' suits and mop-top hairstyles (and of course their comfortable position in mainstream variety performances). These all-pleasing uniforms are worn for every song in the film, the only concession to a rehearsal being John's undone top button. Indeed, the film lightly deflates the force of this distinctive appearance: when Ringo walks out of the group he only has to don a long overcoat and peaked cap to achieve instant anonymity.

Nevertheless, the Beatles' 'look' is shown to be at the forefront of public consciousness, their hair forming by far the most common subject for journalists' questions at the conference: when a society reporter asks Ringo, 'Do you think these haircuts have come to stay?' he replies: 'Well, this one has, you know. It's stuck on good and proper now.' The sticking power and unifying significance of their hairstyle is demonstrated by the publicity poster for the film, and re-enforced in the film's closing credits, when close-up photos of each band member are overlaid on top of one another so quickly that it is almost impossible to differentiate. After main cast and crew credits are laid beside differently posed portraits, final photos are identically framed, with each Beatle's eyes looking upward to the credits printed across their quasi-identical haircuts. 'The End' is printed across the back of George Harrison's head, establishing closure not on any individuality, but on the style: the Beatle mop-top.

There are other instances of the four seeming indivisible, none more so than at the outset when Norm enters their train compartment, points to Paul's grandfather and 'Who's that little old man?' chorus John, Paul, George and Ringo. There are displays of internal conflict, with Ringo getting upset at the others' taunts, but even this functions primarily as a plot device to demonstrate the bonds that constitute the group's special relationship – and to provide some slapstick humour as they rescue Ringo from police custody. On their own, the boys' scenes are more melancholy in tone: isolated, they are more likely to wander into trouble ('He's just a trouble-maker,' says Simon as George leaves; 'On your way, trouble-maker,' the pub landlady yells at Ringo). United, their music and their mischief know no bounds; together, they are 'fun'.

Their togetherness is paralleled in the group of truant schoolchildren that Ringo meets on the canal bank. The lad he meets, Charley, 'a deserter' just like himself, tells him about the rest of his gang. There is

5. *'Charley Peace'. Ringo as Charley (Chaplin).*

Ginger who is 'mad: he says things all the time'; Eddie Fallon who is 'good at spitting and punching'; and finally Ding-Dong (Bell) who is 'a bighead: he fancies himself'. This arrogance is accepted, however, 'coz he's one of the gang'. Group loyalty is more important than personal deficiencies, a message not lost on Ringo as he watches Charley rush down the embankment to rejoin his mates. Later, the police sergeant will call Ringo 'Charley Peace', an apposite sobriquet since the first name ties Ringo narratively to the young boy, and comedically to Chaplin, while the surname connotes the group's social influence. However one judges their attitude towards old and middle age, the Beatles incontrovertibly foster inclusion among the younger generation: when asked at the press conference the topical question of the moment, if he is a mod or a rocker, Ringo's reply that he is 'a mocker' not only demonstrates the Beatles' stance to authority, but purports a synthesis of different young (subcultural) affiliations. The Italian film title 'All for One', for all its Cliff Richard connotations, is far from inappropriate.

Nevertheless *A Hard Day's Night*, with its discrete sequences for each member of the group, went a long way towards establishing their separate personalities in the mind of the public, typecasting them as smart, cute, distant and homely. Especially in America the film helped to transform them from yet another anonymous adolescent package: as Roger Ebert claims, 'after that movie was released everybody knew the names of all four Beatles'.[36] The style of filming and 'acting' made audiences think these were the real Beatles and throughout their careers the stereotype stuck, somewhat to the group's later annoyance. Nevertheless, this individuality was immediately understood as a central part of the recipe of success for the group; though not as cynically manufactured as the boy bands of the 1990s, it was clear that the widespread appeal came from the fact that each member appealed to different sectors of the buying public. Lennon and Harrison, with their cynicism, appealed to older, mainly male fans; McCartney, though the best musician, appealed mainly for his pin-up good looks to the girls; and lovable Ringo, while generally acceptable, appealed particularly to their mums. This 'product variety' had been expounded prior to *A Hard Day's Night* – for example Maureen Cleeve wrote an admired four-part analysis of the group in the *Evening Standard* (17–20 October 1963) – but the film works hard to accentuate these basic character traits – very successfully, to judge from the contemporary reviews. Without ever probing their psychological depths, Owen offers more of the same – Peter Brown and Steven Gaines call them 'cartoon strokes'[37] – allowing the Fab Four to play this 'public' self without impediment.

One tentative division could be made in the characterisations of the four group members. John and Paul dominate the exchanges with the commuter in the train, but thereafter the major 'solo' spots go to George and Ringo: they become the more 'active' members of the film, as evidenced by the group's escape to the disco, where it is George and Ringo who dance, while John and Paul are content to sit and drink and talk to the girls. John and Paul, though, are seen as musically dominant. After their impromptu performance of 'If I Fell', both offer instruction to Ringo. Similarly, after George sings the Lennon and McCartney composition 'I'm Happy Just to Dance with You', John turns to congratulate him: 'Very good that, George.' Paul agrees: 'You're trying.' The comments are all couched in humour but there remains a hint of authority that would later manifest itself more abrasively in *Let It Be* (1970).

The 'musical' duo John and Paul are, as evidenced by the nightclub scenes, more concertedly after the company of women. When they see the schoolgirls on the train, John suggests 'pulling' them, and Paul does the chatting up. When they meet the girls again in the train compartment and John pretends to be an escaped convict, he leers and tells his screaming fans: 'I bet you can guess what I was in for!' When a female journalist is foolish enough to ask John for his hobbies, his written reply succeeds in spooking the bourgeoisie. And for all his gay play

6. 'Day Tripper'. John feeds his Coke habit

he constantly propositions make-up girls and dancers. Paul is equally eager to chase after sex: on the train when John suggests that a carriage might contain a honeymooning couple, Paul nevertheless knocks on the door and enters, claiming: 'I don't care, I'm going to broaden my outlook.' When they discover that his grandfather has gone to the casino it is Paul who suggests that 'he is probably in the middle of an orgy by now' and is the first to rush out of the door in pursuit.

Thereafter, one can find tentative signs of John the social critic. In the baggage van, he sees a cocker spaniel tied up and says, 'Funny, they usually reckon dogs more than people in England.' It's John who suggests Grandfather McCartney would have had a more dignified old age if he had emigrated to America: there he could have been 'a senior citizen of Boston' instead of which he is 'a lonely old man from Liverpool'. It is John who improvises sinking German subs in the bath – a hint of his later partnership with Lester in decrying the infantile insanity of battle in *How I Won the War* (1968). In the film's one drugs reference, it is John who takes a snort, one nostril at a time, from a bottle of Coke (though a close inspection shows it to be a bottle of Pepsi – further duplicity). Above all, it is John who is most openly hostile to those around him: when Paul is trying to reason with the commuter John tells him to 'knock it off. You can't win with his sort. After all, it's his train. Isn't it, Mister?' John threatens one of the actors in the make-up room with 'a punch up your frogged tunic'; John constantly calls Norm a 'swine'. (From the boys on the canal bank John echoes Eddie

Fallon.) Norm rightly sees him as the main agent of rebellion: after telling them to answer their fan mail, John instantly invites the others to follow him out on to the town; at the end, when Norm tells them they are moving straight on to Wolverhampton, it is John who snaps back angrily, ready to refuse. Norm sees all his dilemmas as 'a battle of nerves between John and me'. When Shake points out that John has no nerves, Norm agrees that that's the trouble. 'Sometimes I think he enjoys seeing me suffer,' he says, head in hands. After admitting that he has toyed with the idea of a ball and chain, he adds: 'But he'd just rattle them at me, and in public too.' The word 'rattle' immediately connotes John's impudent advice at the Royal Variety Performance the previous 4 November for the more prestigious members of the audience – i.e. the Queen Mother – to 'rattle their jewellery'. To reinforce the allusion John openly mimics royalty when he cuts a tailor's outstretched measuring tape, declaring in a regally pitched voice: 'I now declare this bridge open.' Finally, John, as all realised even then, was the most 'complex' of the Fab Four – he even cheats his mates at cards, pulling an ace from his sleeve. The doubleness/duplicity that runs throughout the film is highlighted in John's scene with Millie backstage. Not only does he immediately deny who he is, but he is shot leaning against the wall, beside a mirror: the resultant reflection presents a Janus-faced Lennon, untrustworthy, insincere; a doubleness repeated during the filming of 'And I Love Her'.

By comparison Paul has little chance to stamp a personality on the film. Ironically (given one of the explanations for his solo scene being cut), Paul is seen as the classical actor of the group: in the make-up room Paul dons a cape and false nose and starts – accurately – to declaim Shakespeare, with full sweeping gestures and rounded tones: 'O that this too, too solid flesh would melt'. Elsewhere, when not chasing the girls, he cares for his grandfather, combs his hair in the compartment mirror and is often caught in smiling, arc-lit profile (Paul as Ding-Dong).

George, often viewed as 'the quiet one', nevertheless gets the longest lines and longest solo scene. Above all, he conveys a character who is always 'cool' (definitely not 'passionate and right-wing'), unruffled by any occurrence. Early on, when the boys spot the schoolgirls, George warns Paul not to rush: 'None of your five-bar-gate jumps over sort of stuff.' When Paul asks what it means, George says 'I dunno. I just thought it sounded distinguished like.' In the green room before their show, the 'Scouse of Distinction' follows Paul's hammy bit of

7. *'Two-faced Trouble-maker'. John as Janus.*

Shakespeare by turning to one of the make-up girls and saying, calmly: 'Hey, you won't interfere with the basic rugged concept of me personality, will you, madam?' When he finds his way to the style agency and is asked to give his opinion on some shirts, George replies, 'By all means. I am quite prepared for that eventuality' (George as Ginger). George is the most laconic of the Fab Four, though Ringo sees it less positively, advising him to 'stop looking so scornful, it's twisting your face'. This scorn links him most closely with John – and teenage male approval.

Ringo is different. To begin with, as the last arrival in the group, an element of manufacture must here be countenanced. In his analysis of the Beatles, George Melly sees Ringo as an astute replacement for Pete Best: 'Ringo is not the world's most inventive drummer but he is lovably plain, a bit "thick" as a public persona, and decidedly ordinary in his tastes. He acts as a bridge, reassuring proof that the Beatles bear some relation to ordinary people. The Beatles' intuition had told them that ... they needed Ringo.'[38] Owen and Lester also see that need, exploiting Ringo's potential as the *homme moyen sensuel*. Unlike a star surrounded by sycophants, Ringo makes jokes that nobody laughs at. When Paul, asked if his grandfather can talk, says, 'Of course he can, he's a human being!' Ringo pipes up: 'Well, if he's your grandfather, who knows!' and laughs loudly, but alone. Later, when the group catch up with McCartney Senior in the casino and his bill matches his winnings, Ringo laughs again: 'Well, easy come, easy go!' To a man, the others glare at him disapprovingly.

Ringo's 'plainness' is constantly harped on by the others. In their hotel room, George accuses him of snoring. Paul says: 'With a trombone hooter like yours it would be unnatural if you didn't.' Paul's grandfather stirs the situation by reprimanding Paul for mocking the afflicted. 'He can't help having a hideous great hooter.' These comments send Ringo to look at himself in the mirror: the one Beatle to demonstrate dissatisfaction with his physical appearance. The slurs continue: at the press conference we hear John admit, 'I never noticed his nose until about six months ago,' while in the studio canteen, Paul's grandfather begins his 'mixing' by saying: 'Will you look at him sitting there, with his hooter scraping away at that book!'

It is immediately established that Ringo is the scapegoat figure for the group. When they join Paul and his grandfather in the luggage compartment of the train, George says to Ringo, 'Anyway, it's your fault.' 'Why me?' Ringo asks, his voice high-pitched with hurt innocence. 'Why not?' George replies with his trademark indifference. When Paul's grandfather disappears to the casino, Ringo is again blamed, this time for receiving the invite in the first place. The invite came as part of Ringo's fan mail: initially it is the only letter he gets, but seconds later his wider popularity is shown by a separate batch arriving all for him. It gets him no praise from the other boys, though, with John accusing him of writing all the letters himself, while George points out that he has a large family. Even when they run around to 'Can't Buy Me Love' it is Ringo the other three kick at when he is on the ground. Add to this John and Paul's comments on his drumming after they have performed 'If I Fell' expressly to cheer him up, and Ringo is plainly depicted as the Beatle least admired by the others, least contented with his lot.

The objections of his colleagues seem to be grounded in Ringo's more responsible, adult approach to his work – at one stage John calls him 'the middle-aged boy-wonder'. When Norm informs the group that they are wanted in the studio, Ringo says: 'Gear! I'm dying to do a bit of work.' 'God bless you, Ringo,' Norm says, to which the others reply with schoolboy invective. 'Teacher's pet!' says Paul. 'Crawler!' adds George. 'He's betrayed the class,' accuses John, flirting – as was his wont – with social critique. It is hard to disagree with 'Mixer' McCartney when he later observes that the others are 'exploiting your good nature' with 'their cruel unnatural treatment' and they are 'never happy unless they're jeering you'. Ringo is the one Beatle we see reading: he explains to McCartney Senior that 'you can learn from books' and that 'books are good'. However, Paul's grandfather persuades him to live life rather than read it: all he has is 'a bloody book' when he 'could be out there betraying a rich American widow or sipping palm wine in Tahiti before you're too old like me'. Ringo, a bit 'thick' in Melly's words, says, 'Funny, I never thought really, but being middle-aged and old takes up most of your life, doesn't it?' And thus he decides to parade the streets, be young and irresponsible, as he perceives John, Paul and George to be.

But even after he walks out, Ringo is the victim of prejudice, this time from the police, who interpret his various well-intentioned if incompetent actions as 'wandering abroad, malicious intent, acting in a suspicious manner and conduct likely to cause a breach of the peace'. The sergeant refers to him as 'a little savage', while the arresting officer – adding racism to sizeism – says that he is 'probably a little aborigine'. Yet we know that he had only indulged his 'ordinary tastes' by buying a pint of beer and playing a game of darts, had shown empathy for the working-class boy skipping school, and had only been acting the gallant gentleman, laying down his coat so a woman could walk over the puddles on a building site. Unable to realise his ambitions, Ringo is the link, the character with whom the audience can readily identify, unlike the other three, removed by their stardom and musical talent.

However, the doubleness in Ringo's persona places the erudite alongside the 'thick'. When the studio engineer calls him 'arbitrary', he snaps back: 'There you go, hiding behind a smokescreen of bourgeois cliché.' Standing alone in the train corridor he confesses to George that Paul's grandfather does not like him. 'It's because I'm little,' he says and George accuses him of having an inferiority complex. Ringo replies: 'I know. That's why I play the drums. It's my active compensatory factor.' Moments later, a well-dressed woman invites him into her compartment. Ringo counters George's encouragement: 'No, she'll only reject me in the end and I'll be frustrated. I know the psychological pattern. It plays havoc with my drumskins.' This articulate awareness could encourage us to delve into Freudian depths of personal psychoanalysis, but rock critic Richard Meltzer summarises Susan Sontag's argument in *Against Interpretation* that contemporary art should be assessed strictly according to its surface appearance, by the way this appearance denies the critic ground for conventional analysis. Meltzer highlights Ringo's prevarications, and John's dalliance with the pompous commuter, as useful examples of the surplus of Freudian imagery in the popular film, and what happens to Freud when everyone knows a surplus exists: 'Such

ANALYSIS

8. *'Feeling You Holding Me Tight'. Patti meets George, and Freud.*

intentional and obvious psychological references are so blatant as to *be* the surface appearance itself, supplying an explanation itself with no further need to reach below: yet this type of self explanatory surface is such an overstatement that it baffles the analytical critic far more than ordinarily.'[39] Does a knowing humour defuse the actions of schoolgirl Patti Boyd who, as the boys start singing on the train, strokes the phallic handle of an upturned shovel? Should one probe the boys' Lacanian obsession with mirrors? With Meltzer's warning to hand, it is perhaps politic to stick to an analysis of that surface appearance.

TENDING TO BLACK-AND-WHITE THE WHOLE SITUATION

If one examines the look of *A Hard Day's Night*, Lester's cinematic treatment of the Beatles enlists features common to all his 1960s work, innovative camera-work and consciously artistic appropriations. While attracted to the television-influenced style of *cinéma-vérité*, Lester and photographer Gilbert Taylor still sought to play with the aesthetic possibilities of the medium. Taylor underlined the importance of experimenting with the whole range of the black-and-white scale in the presentation of pop acts, first attempted in *It's Trad, Dad!*: 'By using absolutely white backings and a key light we could make the people who played against this "white-out" environment take on the definition of steel engravings.'[40] This method of filming adds a blanched distance to a documentary recording, a visual admission that the celluloid record

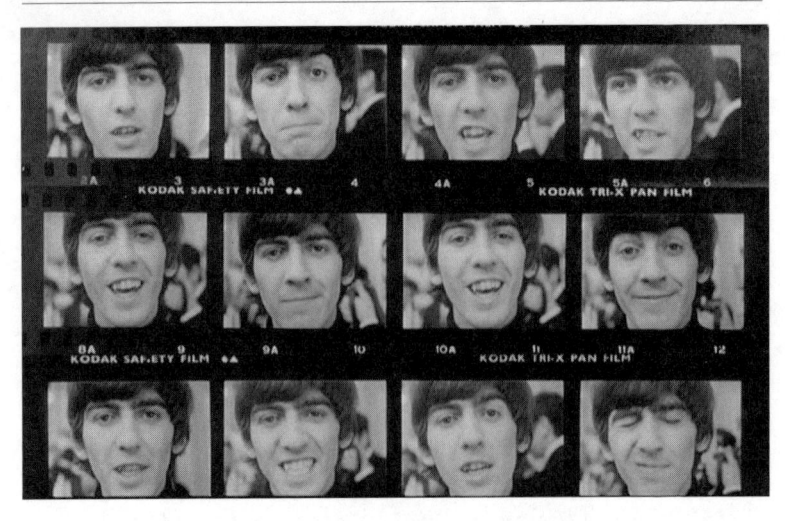

9. *'Pop Art'. Richard + George = Andy + Jackie.*

we watch can hope to reproduce only a simplified version of the liveliness conveyed 'in the flesh': the 'real' energy of the boys 'escapes' celluloid entrapment.

Alongside this technical know-how are placed carefully judged artistic influences. As in *It's Trad, Dad!* Lester strategically employs his knowledge of pop art, but here it privileges liberation above commodification. As the boys make their escape down the fire escape, there are again images of the group shot through a grille similar to that used to film Acker Bilk and his Jazzmen. Here, though, it is a fleeting glimpse from below, a passage to temporary release. The main form employed to catch the image of the moment is freeze-frame photography, a repetition of photographs used during the group's press conference and on the film's publicity poster. It is a device that elicits comparisons with the work of Andy Warhol. Each image is stored, stacked mechanically to emphasise a repetitiousness mirroring of the industrial process that brought the group to public attention in the first place. And yet each shot, though underlining the similarity in the group's dress and hairstyle, is subtly different, again working to individualise the quartet.

With the appearance across and down the screen of the posing George Harrison we see both a Warholian celebration of the visual rhythm of contemporary 'packaging' – the boys are as manufactured as a tin of soup – and, simultaneously, a celebration of variation within standardisation. But the repetition also works with a critical reflexivity evident in a Warhol painting like *Jackie* (1964), his portrait of the widowed Jackie Kennedy. Arguably, the press conference held for the arrival of the Beatles at the newly named Kennedy Airport in February 1964 constituted the biggest media event in the United States since the assassination and funeral of President John F. Kennedy in November 1963. Possibly as much as the shooting, only dimly caught on camera, it was the close-up photos of a grieving Jackie Kennedy that shook the media world and consequently the American people. The smiling, elegantly dressed and coiffeured wife of the President had personified the nation's hopes of a dynamic union between the worlds of politics and culture, hopes that seemed to disappear with the photos of a distraught young widow up to and during the funeral. The relayed black-and-white images of Jackie stunned or in tears destroyed a nation's colourful hopes of freedom, of youthful, fearless leadership that had grown during the Kennedy era. The arrival of the Fab Four can be seen as a significant step in the recovery first of the American media and then of the nation itself. The spirit of Camelot, shot down in Dallas, Texas, had flown over from Liverpool, England, and the unprecedented euphoria that greeted the group seemed part of an expiation, a nation shaking itself out of its state of grief and mourning.

Both periods were given artistic treatment. Andy Warhol returned several times to those images of Jackie Kennedy, mostly, but not exclusively, taking one photographic image and repeating it across different planes of the canvas: Richard Lester, in his re-creation of that Kennedy Airport press conference, similarly centred on still photographic images relayed in patterned strips across the screen. Both works inevitably comment on the power of the electronic media. Eric Shanes notes that Warhol objected strongly to the way television and other media were programming everybody to feel sad, and so reproduced a photograph taken on the evening after John F. Kennedy's assassination.[41] In *A Hard Day's Night* everybody is being 'programmed' to accept the Fab Four's youthful enjoyment and irreverence. Though the emotions are far opposed, both art forms indirectly suggest the processes of programming by the use of a repetitiousness that is metonymic of the way the mass-communications industry disseminates pained or joyous images through a multitude of printed and electronic media to the world. But again, like Warhol, Lester has the best of both worlds, since through the visual rhythm the images approach the condition of abstraction. The emotion is disseminated but ultimately dissipated since, as Klaus Honnof comments on Warhol, 'continual reiteration undermines the exceptional nature of the original subject matter. Its uniqueness is dissolved by virtue of repetition, it loses its contours, fades and by fading brings into force a world cloaked by the constant barrage of the mass media.'[42]

We consume the image, but the real person escapes us. Walter Spies wrote of Warhol rendering the desolation of repetition, 'the destruction of feeling by overexposure and of enjoyment by consumption'.[43] Such is the case in *A Hard Day's Night* which, while filming the celebrity imprisonment of the band, highlights the medium's inability to 'capture' the four young individuals behind the fashionable façade. Throughout, the film makes great play with reflections rather than reality: Paul preens himself in a train mirror; Ringo checks on the size of his nose; George shaves the reflection of Shake's face on the hotel bathroom mirror; Millie turns John's face to the theatre mirror in an attempt to reveal his true identity. Such play with image over reality parallels the film's proliferation of photos, television shots and stage designs. For Jon Lewis, the group's 'inaccessibility is held up as the logical extension of stardom: the scrapbook of images is as close to them as we will ever get. Stylistically, Lester demystifies stardom; thematically he glorifies it.'[44] And yet, illustrating again the film's core duality, one could just as easily reverse Lewis's conclusion: Lester and Taylor's appropriation of pop art, photography and even *cinéma-vérité* contribute to star construction, while the frantic action and gnomic utterances only serve to demonstrate that for all the plot's drive to re-present the group's imprisonment the Fab Four remain beyond our grasp, unknowable, as distant to our understanding as their on-stage 'white-out' background.

BACKSTAGE POLITICS

The dualities of the film text as well as the (attempted) duplicities of the film-makers and the Beatles are evident in *A Hard Day's Night*'s generic characteristics – both documentary realism and musical comedy. The film's claims to present a 'realistic' insight to life on the road for the Beatles are *partially* supported by a comparison with the concurrent documentary shot by the American independent film-makers Albert and David Maysles. Granada Television commissioned the Maysles brothers to record the impact of the Beatles on their breakthrough tour of the United States in February 1964. Contractual difficulties meant that the film was never shown in its original format and only New York footage was used for *Yeah! Yeah! Yeah! New York Meets the Beatles*, broadcast on 12 February 1964 in Britain, while a fuller treatment, retitled *The Beatles in America* (aka *What's Happening! The Beatles in the USA*) was aired on 13 November on CBS in America. The limited release of this project must have been much to United Artists' relief since a number of the scenes filmed were very similar to *A Hard Day's Night*. The Maysles documentary records the Kennedy Airport press conference, the hotel and car sieges, even a train journey and escape to a nightclub, plus of course interspersed footage of performances to a chorus of hysterical fans. There are significant differences, though, between the two products: the 'genuine' documentary shows a social realism by providing evidence of the 'real' public and private side to life on tour: not just the performances, but the relentless and ruthless hawking of wares to radio stations; not only the smoking and drinking, but also the girls being smuggled into their rooms late at night. By contrast, Lester's version can appear more as a socialist (capitalist?) realist tract – propaganda for the stars of pop.

A Hard Day's Night is, of course, an invented – and sanitised – version of events and so it is perhaps unfair to push too far a comparison with avowed documentary practice. What, though, of its similarities with contemporary fictional practices? Bob Neaverson, for example, sees the film as a 'cinematic bastard', but stresses how 'Lester and Owen's narrative construction and pacing is, in effect (if not intention), closer to that of the French "new wave" than to any previous British or American pop musical.'[45] Lester was an avowed admirer of the work of French new wave directors such as Jean-Luc Godard and François Truffaut and comments on his use of new-wave techniques in the video *You Can't Do That: The Making of A Hard Day's Night*. From the film's opening chase sequence one is struck by the technical parallels, the use of a hand-held camera, swish pans and jump-cuts.

Nevertheless, as contemporary film critics noted, several of these mostly comic effects connote the silent movie practice of Chaplin and Keaton as much as if not more than the *Cahiers du Cinéma* cohort. Ringo's solo spot is replete with 'Chaplinesque' moments: sitting alone at the river's edge, he places his camera on a boulder in order to photograph himself, but when he snaps the shutter cord the camera springs back into the water; when he enters the pub he sprays his change across a game of shove halfpenny, places his glass on a bar skittles game where it is immediately smashed, and then tries to play darts, his first arrow landing in another customer's sandwich, his second in the landlady's parrot cage; he tries to imitate Sir Walter Raleigh by draping his raincoat over a muddy path for the benefit of a young lady, only to send her plummeting into a head-high hole. Finally, the freeing of Ringo from police custody gives us – as in Cliff Richard's *Wonderful Life* – a lengthy homage to the Keystone Kops. Other sight gags have a more surreal slant: Norm looking for John Lennon down the plughole of his emptied bath; George teaching Shake how to wet-shave on the mirror. For a film originating with the US market in mind, *A Hard Day's Night* appears to make few concessions to the American sense of humour if one thinks of the Goons as the predominant comic mentors of such moments of mayhem. Lennon clearly saw this comedic provenance as part of the group's stance of resistance: 'We were the sons of the Goon Show. We were of an age. We were the extension of that rebellion in a way.'[46] Lester, however, early in the film, seems consciously to 'clue in' the American viewer to the type of humour being used, as the camera dwells on Shake reading a copy of Walter S. Gaines's *Son of Mad*. A vein of verbal humour reminiscent of Laurel and Hardy is provided by Norm and Shake, with Norm criticising his dim-witted partner for always being taller than he is. Like Grandfather McCartney and his Steptoe connotations, these older actors provide a more mainstream comedy, a middle ground between the Beatles' Keatonesque routines and Goon-like repartee.

For all its comedic innovation and quotation, however, it needs to be stressed that the Beatles' first movie must also be read as a traditional musical comedy imbued with Hollywood conventions. In *Hollywood UK* Alun Owen says: 'Instead of doing "We're all going on a summer's [sic] holiday", with all that lovely lighting, no ... really gritty' and the programme moves to Owen from a clip of Cliff driving his London double-decker bus.[47] Yet the choice of that one film is disingenuous since, as much as Cliff's earlier *The Young Ones* and his concurrent *Wonderful Life*, *A Hard Day's Night* functions primarily as a backstage musical and through its formulae we are allowed access both to the public and private lives of the stars. This was a tried and trusted strategy, well suited to the production company's aims of demonstrating the Beatles' confident musicianship and differentiating their individual personalities. In essence, the film *is* about putting on a show, and not a pure pop or rock transmission. In a move no different from that undertaken by Tommy Steele and Cliff Richard, the Beatles top the bill of a variety show, a bill including Lionel Blair and his dancers, operetta singers, even Derek Nimmo and his performing doves. (As Michael Braun reports on their January tour of France: 'Shortly after midnight the Beatles were introduced, but then a juggling act came on stage.')'[48]

Nevertheless, within this established sub-genre, there are two ways in which *A Hard Day's Night* demonstrates its advance on previous pop musicals – and registers its inherent modernity. The first is by removing this backstage show from a theatrical, or even cinematic context, as had been the case for Tommy, Cliff and others. As in *It's Trad, Dad!* we are here thrust into the electronic – and at the time innovative, generally unknown – processes of live television transmission. It is a further duality: a traditional backstage musical set in the white heat of technology. We see the Beatles constantly mediated through a camera viewfinder or control-room monitors as the new medium of television is everywhere foregrounded and fetishised. It is an apposite presentation, since television was the familiar medium of the Beatles: their fan base had already grown due to their televised appearances on just such variety shows – 15 million watching them top the bill on *Sunday Night at the London Palladium* (13 October 1963) while 26 million saw their appearance on the *Royal Variety Performance* (4 November 1963). It had also been their passport to acceptance in America, and their 73 million audience on the *Ed Sullivan Show* (9 February 1964). With the editing drawing attention to its use of multiple cameras, with such cameras often present in shot, we are aware how everything concerning the foursome is electronically orchestrated: they are revealed as versatile performers whose performance is universalised by the newly dominant and dexterous medium. The Beatles were the first group to be marketed through television: the film of *A Hard Day's Night* does not upset that successful strategy.

The second 'modernist' strategy employed is what Janet Feuer has termed a critical reflexivity. Feuer notes how self-reflexivity as a critical category has been associated with aesthetically or politically radical films, such as those of Godard, which call attention to the codes constituting their own signifying practices and interrogate or 'deconstruct' their own narrativity. The last film of the Cliff Richard musical trilogy, *Wonderful Life*, released a week prior to *A Hard Day's Night*, is also a film about the filming of musical numbers, yet its random quotation and pastiche of the past Hollywood tradition invests it with a more 'conservative reflexivity',[49] a display and dependence on the pattern of historical succession in the attempt to revisit and revivify rather than break open past generic forms. During the song 'On the Beach' the Shadows make a musical quotation from 'Twist and Shout', a (futile) attempt to hang on to the coat tails of the newly popular Merseybeat sound. When John Lennon cries out, 'Hey kids, I've got a great idea. Why don't we do the show right here?' he is deliberately distancing the Beatles' film from the Rooney–Garland-inspired product of Cliff and the Shadows. At the same time John is exposing the structure itself at the expense of a transparent transfer of the ritual value contained within the genre.

And yet, by consciously mocking conventions, has John bitten off more than he can chew? For while a western or horror film can move relatively smoothly to parody, contestation and even deconstruction, this is problematical in a genre whose explicit function is to glorify the world of entertainment while being itself an example of that entertainment. Lennon was upset that people did not see sufficiently the irony of his pronouncement, even though its motivation seemed explicitly to be the Sahara-set rival Richard vehicle.

> It was a joke originally that we threw in. Norman Rossington said it used to happen in all the old pop films. They'd be in the middle of a desert and somebody would say, 'I've got a great idea, kids, how about doing the show right here?' I stuck that bit in but it doesn't work; it looks as though I meant it.[50]

If the joke fails to ring entirely true, this is because it is easier for other genres to become increasingly self-critical or socially critical without having to confront the dilemma of criticising mass entertainment itself. Lennon's own film effort can afford to be cynical about entertainment just as long as it is still providing that entertainment in the process. His director gives it to us *as* the process, but in a form still readable as spontaneous performance: for all the group's critical irony, the film still ends with the boys putting on the show. Lennon, duplicitous as ever, is having his generic cake and eating it, as *A Hard Day's Night* adopts an ironic distance from the plot structures of the backstage musical, but entertains a broad family audience by using those very structures. Thus one can detect in the film's variety structure and verbal surrealism a clear lineage dating back, as John Mundy notes, to *Elstree Calling* (1930), the Crazy Gang vehicle *Okay for Sound* (1937) and Tommy Handley's *It's That Man Again* (1943).[51] It will be left to Jean-Luc Godard and the Rolling Stones, in *One Plus One* (1968), to take the genre further still and dismantle the expected group finale.

ANALYSIS

MUSICAL ARRANGEMENT ... PICTURE-WISE

What of that musical content? Do the Beatles present us with a music of rebellion? Yes and no, has to be the response, with a doubleness again evident in the discourse. For George Melly the Beatles' songs at that time 'trapped what it felt like to be a rebellious suburban Liverpudlian for whom beat music offered an escape. They were tough *and* tender. You could sense, behind the words and music, the emergence of a new spirit: post-war, clever, nonconformist, and above all cool.'[52] This coexistence of the tough and the tender can vary in emphasis from song to song – the film showcases the Beatles' established musical versatility from ballads like 'And I Love Her' to faster pop numbers such as 'Can't Buy Me Love' – but there is little sense of a *contrast* of styles, as was so markedly apparent in the Cliff Richard musicals.

One can, though, make a broad division in what must, overall, be seen as a music of transition. Wilfrid Mellers has described early Beatles' compositions such as 'Love Me Do' and 'I Saw Her Standing There' as 'edenic', songs of growing up where 'the tune matches the innocence of the words, for it springs from the very origins of primitive song'.[53] There are examples in the movie, such as 'I'm Happy Just to Dance with You' and the disco track 'I Wanna Be Your Man', described by Mellers as 'one of the most primitive'.[54] But songs such as the film's title-track signify a change. Although it is still a love song, 'a more "experienced" quality is evident in the verses, which use less youthfully abstract jargon, more down to earth fact', as evidenced by phrases such as 'working like a dog'. Mellers draws attention to sexual innuendo in the delivery of 'things' and 'feel all right' and highlights 'the division between innocence (the ecstasy of being "held tight") and experience (things, making money, the tedium of work ...)'.[55] Similarly, 'If I Fell' is another mature, adult love song, one that discusses the experience of a former, unsuccessful relationship, 'a song not only about love, but also about responsibility'[56] – one could add that in the second line it has a vulnerable plea that assists an understanding of the following year's more open plea for 'Help!'. Such songs match their lyrical richness with a concomitant musical maturity: as Ian MacDonald notes, the material on *A Hard Day's Night* 'shows an interest in tonal ambiguity which contrasts markedly with earlier Beatles' key schemes'.[57] Also, as an LP largely written by Lennon, the soundtrack 'offers the richest harvest of implied harmonies of any single Beatles collection'.[58]

What then of the way in which this music is incorporated into Lester's cod-documentary? Although it is for the most part conventionally motivated, the grammar of cinematic correlation again does much to advance the British pop musical to a new level of sophistication. This is not so much the case for the opening number, since the rolling of the credits as the Beatles run for cover is no different in concept from Cliff and the Shadows sailing for sanctuary at the start of *Wonderful Life*. We later realise, though, that unlike Cliff's musicals, this opening has signalled that the film will repeatedly employ musical numbers without tying them to musical performance. When completed we also understand that it enhances the sense of routine and repetition that the film tries to convey. 'A Hard Day's Night' is played over both the opening and end credits to give the film a circular structure: this musically re-enforces the meaning given by Norm's orders to move on for their next 'midnight matinee'; it provides a sonic confirmation that the thirty-six hours we have just seen will go on and on and on. The song's own structure reiterates this circularity, ending with a repeated arpeggio that outlines the same notes from the opening chord as the song and helicopter blades spin into fade-out.

A break with the conventions of musical presentation is more immediately noticeable during the first number in the carriage, 'I Should Have Known Better'. Having started to sing while playing cards, the boys' cards are suddenly – surreally – transformed into musical instruments, only to return to a hand of cards as the song enters its final chorus. Acting as a vital signpost to the duality rampant in *A Hard Day's Night*, the presentation of 'I Should Have Known Better' both is and is not diegetic, thus rupturing any reading of the film as generically coherent and inducting us into an overall viewing strategy. Its effect is akin to the Brechtian stacked musicians in *It's Trad, Dad!* and, coupled with the earlier 'surreal' high-jinks where the group taunt the commuter outside the train, the cinematic correlation advocates a move towards alterity, generic hybridity, a constitutive duplicity. It is also thoroughly democratic, ensuring that all four Beatles receive equivalent group and solo exposure. Vocalist John is privileged for seven shots during the song, but Paul, Ringo and George are each seen in close-up three times (four for George if one includes a close-up on his guitar work). This indicates a new emphasis for a new phenomenon: the filming never prioritises the singer above the corporate instrumentalism – the music, as the life, is conveyed as 'all for one'. Finally, the decor, with wire fencing both protecting and imprisoning, shows the song to be a bridge to later performances: as Alun Owen commented, 'The only freedom they ever get is when they start to play their music and then their faces

ANALYSIS

10. *'I Work All Day'. Music as Labour.*

light up and they're happy; but mostly they're confined.'[59] Here, they appear momentarily happy in their confinement.

The next number, 'If I Fell', is again conventionally motivated, though delivered with a twist. If the Hollywood musical established the trope of a stage rehearsal passing for a finished performance, here the spontaneity instigated by John makes no attempt to mask the rehearsal process. Yes, the lip-synched song is delivered without audible accident, but on stage all around them is rough and ready. This number is an act of preparation, the initial placement of the Beatles' performances in a context of mediation. After early shots of John and Ringo, we move to a view down on to the group from above the overhead lighting: here we are given access to the activity behind the group, a floor sweeper and four men setting up the black-and-white hexagonal stands for the stage decor. We then move to a view from behind the group, where we see a stepladder being removed and the camera crew checking their positions. As John sits beside Ringo to sing the second verse we see the cases behind John dislodged as a man runs through some electric cable. Throughout the performance stage crew are walking behind the Beatles. Even when the camera is close up on the group we note some disengagement from the performance, Paul for instance glancing over at the activity to his right. At one point a figure walks right in front of the camera, blacking out the image for a moment. Shake comes on to the stage to adjust the position of George's amp: demonstrating typical proficiency, seconds later the amp crashes off its stand. As the song ends another high shot down from the lighting locates the group amid cameras and booms while, behind them, two men are looking at plans for the stage layout. Unlike Hollywood convention, and the Cliff Richard trilogy, the song is shown in such a way as to foreground its origins in labour and in technology – of which the Beatles themselves form a part. For like the men in the background seeking visual perfection with their floor plan, John turns to Ringo and comments, 'I'd like a little more drums there,' pointing to the drum kit. Paul agrees, adding more instruction: 'On the third bit – more bang!' he says, before demonstrating the required beat with some guitar chords and foot stomping. This debriefing to Ringo re-enforces the point that there is nothing here of the joys of being an amateur. While a film like *Wonderful Life* will set up a contrast between the fun-loving kids doing it for love and the older humourless professionals, 'If I Fell' is a romantic ballad unequivocally positioned as a tested industrial product.

Diametrically opposed to this is the filming to accompany 'Can't Buy Me Love', generally considered to be the finest single sequence in the film. For Neil Sinyard 'it is memorable for the sheer bounce of the number and the way camera and performance combine to create a definitive short ballet of youthful high spirits'.[60] It is a perfect union where Lester and the Beatles indulge to the full their capacity to improvise and show off with and to the camera. It constitutes the single moment of breakthrough for the pop music film: just as the Beatles break out of their incarceration, so is the musical number freed from its generic restrictions; as the boys chase themselves far from the conventions of diegetic performance, they allow the films that follow to employ the pop song as 'traditional' instrumental music had always worked, as an enhancement to the mood of a scene. Here also is the most complete example of Richard Lester's empathy with the music: his creation of a visual correlative to the emotion contained in McCartney's composition. The Beatles' success has deprived them of the simple pleasures enjoyed by others: running mad in a field with your mates, unnoticed by the public and the media, is the emotional equivalent of the 'love' that money just can't buy.

An important factor in the success of the sequence itself is its preparation and context. Until this moment, exactly one-third of the way through the movie, the Beatles have been chased, caged and castigated. Stuck in trains, cars, hotel rooms, even a dimly lit nightclub, there has been a constant sense of claustrophobia. Thus structurally the song represents a massive release of pent-up energies, a chance to stretch

ANALYSIS

11. *'Free as a Bird'*. The escape into non-performative illustration.

out and let go, unseen by prying eyes or pawing hands. Norm, again displeased at the group's antics, is taking them back to their dressing room with the threat of lock and key. Ringo then notices a door marked 'Fire Escape' and nods to the others. The camera registers the white paint of the word 'Escape' as the boys grab their chance and make a dash for freedom. 'We're out!' shouts Ringo, arms raised in triumph. The word on the door has acted like a signal, and they dash down the metal staircase and on to the field below.

As the Beatles cavort in Goon-like release from the rigours of convention, Lester uses varied angles and speeds to convey the energy of the quartet. As they descend the four-storey fire escape we cut three times from the boys on the stairs to a view upwards of the metal grille platform – its Lichtenstein-like circular patterning now signalling porousness rather than imprisonment. As they reach *terra firma* and jump over discarded props, the film momentarily speeds up to help them run and stumble their way into the open air. An aerial shot down on the square concrete heli-pad follows one of the boys down a long path and a full-speed dash back into the centre of the square. The run leads to no special sight gag – it is the expenditure of energy itself that matters, the sense of achieved release. Another Beatle now runs out with jerky, leaping motions before collapsing to the grass. We cut to ground level and the marked-out lanes of an athletics track. Paul raises an imaginary starting pistol, but in their brief access to anarchy the boys stick neither to their lanes nor any agreed running style: within seconds they all collapse as if shot, Paul included. Another aerial shot has the boys back on the concrete square, one in each corner. In pairs they run to the centre and twirl around each other back towards their starting point, a heli-pad highland fling. The filming now gets in there amid the mayhem: as indifferent to rules of acting as they were to athletics, we see Paul run up to and into the camera, grimacing out at us as he breaks the ultimate taboo. A subjective camera sees the feet of two supposed Beatles dancing: this turns to a medium shot of fighting as John downs Ringo and the others join in for a good kicking of the grounded drummer. When Ringo rises, the others drop as if pole-axed. An aerial tracking shot sees the boys running across the field, so fast they trip and fall. Next a slow-motion shot sees John, Paul and George jumping from a height down to the ground; Ringo, on the ground, prepares to move in the reverse direction: he leaps just inches from the ground. This slow interpolation allows time to note how it again enacts the Beatles' existing photographic iconography, in particular Dezo Hoffmann's shot from Liverpool's Sefton Park of the group leaping in the air, the image superimposed on a bombsite background that was used the previous year as the cover of the 'Twist and Shout' EP. A further aerial shot sees another arching dash, only this time the runner has his jacket pulled up over his head. A close-up has three of the group lying head to head on the concrete (Lennon was away that day at a Foyles' literary lunch for *In His Own Write*, a product later carefully placed on the shelf in the boys' changing room), before we cut to a final shot from the air as the foursome run and leapfrog. And rest.

Their fun is abruptly ended, however, as a large middle-aged man appears, dressed in raincoat and wellingtons. As well as tying the number to the train scene with the pompous and territorial commuter, the groundsman's role is identical to that of the policeman at the end of Gene Kelly's 'Singin' in the Rain' routine: he is the representative of elderly authority that will not accept such Dionysian exhibitions of self-abandon. 'I suppose you know this is private property,' he states officiously, expounding propriety to go along with property. 'Sorry we hurt your field, Mister,' George answers, his play on words again conflating fun and trouble, but also emphasising a misplaced prioritising of real estate over ready emotion. There is, though, a further resonance in the groundsman's reprimand, since it is the treatment of the Beatles as *public* property ('moveable property' in Owen's terms) that has prompted their flight. Within *A Hard Day's Night*, 'Can't Buy Me Love' is later

12. *'Tell Me What You See'. Music plus mediation.*

reprised to accompany the manic comedy of the Keystone Kops chase sequence, and the tension between public figures and private spaces is revisited in Lester's later films. Here, though, it motivates the Beatles' own 'Running, Jumping and Standing Still Film'.

Less than three minutes later we are back indoors for a technical rehearsal: director Spinetti's one instruction to the group – 'try not to jiggle out of position' – gives a further justification to the al fresco frolics that we have just witnessed. Now there are rules to obey: we see the group waiting for the tannoyed command 'Music!' before beginning 'And I Love Her'. The establishment shot of the staged performance is straightforward. The hexagonal blocks are now in place and Paul stands in the foreground on a black block with microphone stand in front of him. To his right George stands on the studio floor, his left leg raised to the block so that he can rest his acoustic guitar on his thigh. In the background, between the two, Ringo sits on a higher platform. John is sitting on one of the blocks, in mid-shot over to Paul's left. After the opening bar of George's intro, however, we switch, not to a conventional close-up, but to a screen within a screen, a tighter view of the opening shot that eliminates John. We have moved to the inside of the control room and what follows will exhibit the full extent of the mediation of the Beatles and their music. The monitor switches to a close-up of the excluded John and then, as Paul begins to sing, cuts unexpectedly to George's final notes on the guitar.

The monitor next cuts back to its first tight shot of Paul, George and Ringo. The film camera then pans to the left to reveal a bank of four control room monitors. A hand in the foreground adjusts the volume mix. The film camera then tilts up to view the group through the glass of the control room. For the first time we have the expected focus on the lead singer, but this is only by chance, since the others are obscured by a studio camera and stage floor monitor. After such a fragmented, disorientating presentation, the start of the second verse sees a brief return to the establishment shot. As the middle eight begins we fade to Ringo on the bongos, before another fade takes us back to an oblique angle on three of the control room monitors. Two of these now hold close-ups of Paul, the furthest left cutting different views of George. We fade back out to the studio and an 'unmediated' close-up of Paul's left profile. When George begins his guitar solo, we again move from the musical focus, cutting first to Ringo and then to John, the unfathomable Lennon's image duplicated in the shiny surface of the hexagonal stand in front of him. As before, the close-up of George catches only a few of his final notes, the camera dwelling instead on a close-up of the photogenic Paul. The camera now circles to Paul's left so that, as he sings how 'our love will never die', an arc light shines directly into the lens and the image temporarily 'whites out' before it refocuses on Paul in profiled splendour. United Artists apparently questioned this 'amateurish' shot: Lester again was breaking the cinematic rules, revealing the artifice of performance. A high angle looks down on the group as the final bars are played. This camera then zooms out slowly, and we see, around the group, two booms, one hand-operated, three floor cameras, a monitor, trails of wire and three rows of overhead lighting. We have witnessed, in Walter Benjamin's phrase, 'the work of art in the age of mechanical reproduction'.

Another three minutes later, after being sent downstairs to be 'powdered off, with a shine' the boys are back on stage, this time with their make-up girls in tow as surrogate audience. The Lionel Blair dancers are performing to a piano arrangement of 'I'm Happy Just to Dance with You'. John decides they'll do the show right here and the Beatles perform their original version of the song. This number serves to synthesise the theatrical and televisual effects separately emphasised in the previous two numbers. Though an impromptu performance, the group are still heavily mediated, the song beginning with an establishment shot framed through the viewfinder of the front camera. As we track back we see another duplication, the group both in and behind the viewfinder.

This reverses the movement from 'And I Love Her', changing from the camera's cropped frame to a wider view that returns John to the ensemble. Group positions too are reversed, with Ringo's back now in the foreground, an arrangement that would never be allowed during a bona fide shooting session. The filming tries out further experiments, manipulating our attention from George to John and back again, not by cutting but by placing both in shot and effecting a change of focus. But alongside this cinematic discourse, during the number we see Lionel Blair in the background rehearsing a few steps with his dancers, thus relocating the Beatles in a traditional, variety show format. As the number concludes, we have our first shot from behind the group, revealing two other cameras, with their operators trying out lenses and positions. Again we are made aware of the labour context that permits the filmed spectacle.

This number, though, is distinctive for its artistic design, the occasion for visual punning as behind the Lionel Blair dancers and then the Beatles we see a series of blown-up photographic images of insects. It is exactly the kind of play on word and image that Max Ernst would later attempt in his 1968 Beatles sketches.[61] It is also another example of the film's intent to allow each Beatle to display his individual talents, with 'I'm Happy Just to Dance with You' giving George his turn at singing the lead vocal. Again, though, the camera does not dwell disproportionately on the singer. Diversity with unity is present within each filmed performance as it is in the film as a whole.

(To extend this 'democratic urge' to Ringo needs some special pleading: he can be heard singing 'I Wanna Hold Your Hand' during the disco sequence in the nightclub which, as if in an act of compensation, focuses on Ringo's dancefloor moves. Also, the musical number after 'I Want to Hold Your Hand' concentrates on Ringo wandering the streets to the accompaniment of a string arrangement of 'This Boy' – itself a Top 50 US hit for George Martin.)

The film concludes in conventional fashion with the group in concert. The climax repeats the format of *The Tommy Steele Story*, *The Young Ones* and *It's Trad, Dad!* but the forum has altered considerably. Francis Wheen notes how 'the Beatles resembled Tommy Steele both in the speed of their success – from obscurity to Royal Variety Performance in one year – and in their ability to appeal equally to mums and teenagers'.[62] But Steele was mostly filmed singing to the older generation. The teenage mass hysteria expunged from Steele's cinematic performance is predominant in the Beatles' show – a television booking, but (presented as) filmed in front of a live studio audience. Now we can finally see and hear what Trevor Philpott missed from the Boy from Bermondsey, the 'killing day at some fantastic piggery'.[63] Even before the music starts the camera dwells on the young audience that fills the lower and upper balconies.

Here is the first concerted examination of the relationship between fans and pop. In their discussion of the Beatles' fans in 1964 and 1965, Ehrenreich, Hess and Jacobs argue that the phenomenon of Beatlemania was a form of *sexual* revolution. They see the hysteria replicated by Lester as a protest by young women, if unarticulated, against the confines of the culture in which they have been raised. In their argument, largely centred on Beatlemania in the United States, this hysteria was of a far greater intensity than earlier fan movements such as those of Elvis Presley or Frank Sinatra. Beatlemania in the United States broke out in a middle-class, white culture whose gender roles were severely structured and where sex still came after marriage. The authors argue that the Beatles' appeal centred on their inaccessibility, the fact that the young girl knew that she would never marry or even meet one of them. 'Adulation of the male star was a way to express sexual yearnings that would normally be pressed into the service of popularity or simply repressed.'[64] Beatlemania was made possible in large part by this mode of sexual repression. But this emotion must be interpreted in its social context and the interaction between fans and Beatles was fed, in the authors' argument, by the development of a teenage consumer culture in the United States. Rock'n'roll was central to this culture, which marketed a form of 'hysteria' that could be employed to sell fan merchandise. Thus, the arrival of the Beatles in America was carefully orchestrated, the passion being stoked by press and radio reports of the Beatlemania that had just swept Britain.

This anticipation and inaccessibility is enacted in microcosm in the 'climax' to *A Hard Day's Night*. The concert begins with an excitement-building delayed entry: there are shots of girls screaming, and a view from the back of the stalls that shows how distant and indistinct the stage appears. Then the opening chords of 'Tell Me Why' are rhythmically matched by a close-up of four background posters – each a multiple exposure of a Beatle jumping. The pose on these large rectangular 'pop portraits' is very similar to the jumps seen during the group's escapades in the field behind the studio, a repetition that invites us momentarily to step back from the film narrative and hypothesise that even their moment of escape has been caught and commodified. Another

13. *'She Loves You'. The climax, as boy meets girl.*

view down on to the balcony leads into four separate close-ups of individual fans, each clearly mouthing, in order, 'Paul', 'Ringo', 'John' and 'George'. It is only after this democratic presentation of frieze and frenzy, a full fifteen seconds into the singing of the chorus, that the film presents a shot of the boys on stage. The montage of jumping poses further serves to emphasise the group's distinctively static poses during performance (q.v. the Shadows). First we see a close-up of Paul and George, singing from the same microphone stage left, and then John, stage right. We then return to the audience, for a close-up of first a teary then a dreamy-eyed teenage girl. A close-up of Ringo and shots of John, then Paul and George together, change at the start of the second verse to a shot from the control room. Now the camera looks out to the right, encompassing both the bank of monitors and the tiers of screaming Beatles' fans. A close-up on a fan close to fainting, and more shots of Paul and George, then John, are followed by a slow tracking shot behind Ringo's drums, which presents for the first time both the group and their fans. It is the crowning moment in *A Hard Day's Night*. Lacking the traditional romantic sub-plot, the final 'boy–girl' union is now seen to be that of exultant fans and excited players: within the agreed perimeters of the stage and auditorium, the concert provides a clear exposition of the giving and receiving of the Gospel according to John, Paul, George and Ringo.

John Mundy records how *A Hard Day's Night* adopts 'an almost ethnographic approach' to a phenomenon central in the reconstruction of mid-1960s British identity, especially in the way Lester's 'hand-held' aesthetic 'implicates its young audience within a world which seems occupied as much by themselves as by the Beatles'.[65] 'The love you take is equal to the love you make,' Paul sang on *Abbey Road*, a symbiotic relationship generously recorded by Lester's filming. During the sweeps across the audience, the camera will rest four times on a round-faced blonde, her cheeks streaked with tears. Lester has referred to her as 'the white rabbit',[66] an affectionate sobriquet for a young woman whose own nervous pleasure is given up to the four men she will no doubt continue to follow for the rest of their career and beyond. In the same way that the filming of the Beatles has emphasised the corporate nature of their music, this young woman seems to have lost all sense of personal identity: she is part of a wave of adulation, maddeningly distant from the figures on stage and yet their necessary completion. What she is not, though, is a victim. Ehrenreich, Hess and Jacobs seek to tell us why she, and thousands of others, cry and argue for a doubleness in the new, rock-centred consumer society. For while it sought to manipulate the consumer, it simultaneously structured a teenage culture which was opposed to the adult world, especially subversive of some of its dominant modes of sexuality. 'For girls, fandom offered a way not only to sublimate romantic and sexual yearnings but to carve out subversive versions of heterosexuality.'[67] For these authors, the Beatles expressed a form of playful sexuality that was shocking in the context of the dominant American codes, allowing an opening for the development of alternative roles for women during the later 1960s.

This analysis is refined by L. Grossberg, who distinguishes two types of sensibility at work in phenomena such as Beatlemania. The first is the 'sensibility of the consumer', the most widespread way of interacting with popular culture, and which 'operates by producing structures of pleasure'.[68] The second sort of sensibility is engaged in by the fan, and for Grossberg this operates in the domain of 'affect or mood'. He draws the following distinction: 'Affect is not the same as either emotions or desires. Affect is closely tied to what we often describe as the feeling of life'[69] similar in many ways to Barthes's distinction between the 'rational' kinds of pleasure or '*plaisir*' and the explosions of '*jouissance*'. Grossberg argues that these explosive affects matter: they help us to live in contemporary society, and structure our identity. We see that affect on the face of the 'white rabbit'. She is not just a consumer, she is a fan. She is not just the passive creature condemned by the Frankfurt

School approach; she is fully active in her relationship to text. *A Hard Day's Night* registers and shares her productivity.

Omitting the final chorus of 'Tell Me Why', the film next segues into a concert performance of 'If I Fell'. The opening verse this time is edited out and we cut again from Ringo to the pairing of Paul and George. The shot of John is from a new, low angle, though John's guitar robs the image of the fully provocative and priapic. Creating a résumé of previous visual effects, this number again includes a shot from inside the control room, another profile of Paul that fades to white against the stage lights, and a view from low left of Ringo's drums that underlines the symbiotic nature of the Beatles' stage performance.

Before the final word of the final verse, the concert again segues, this time into the second verse of 'I Should Have Known Better'. Additions here include a view out from the front of the stage, placing two cameras plus operators before the screaming fans, while a high shot down from the lights blanches the Beatles below, an effect repeated by adjusting the monitors in the control room. Here we see extreme close-ups of John's mouth, the fetishising technique used to film Del Shannon in *It's Trad, Dad!*, again appropriate to a song of self-absorption. With a final shot from behind Ringo to re-establish the unity of spectacle, we see the group take a bow and a series of sweeps alight on fans crying, screaming, swooning. The last of these highlights young boys contributing to the general pandemonium.

After these edited versions of three new numbers the set climaxes with the old favourite and signature tune, 'She Loves You'. The number is a simple statement of affirmation, an ode not to rebellion but to joy. And here the Beatles abandon the first person singular to become the spokesmen for encouraging others. Both textually and contextually, it is the only viable concluding number. The song, released back in August 1964, would remain, with one and a half million sales, the group's most successful single in the UK and by the time of filming was already being viewed as a landmark recording. It had been chosen by the group to bring their set to an end when they appeared on ITV's *Sunday Night at the London Palladium* the previous October. The crowd disturbances outside and the reaction inside made the front pages of the national press, events commonly acknowledged as starting the 'youthquake' later christened 'Beatlemania'. *A Hard Day's Night* knows not to mess with that running order.

It also provides the answer to the question one could ask at the film's beginning: why are these young fans behaving like this? In a film that

14. *'You Know My Name'. The consummate professionals, professing instant and copious consumption.*

begins with the effects of Beatlemania, it ends with its single definable cause. One could push the structural closure further: the opening shots show a rush towards a railway carriage, and so, for Tim Riley, does its final number. 'Ringo's opening tom-tom fill that is "She Loves You"'s first sound doesn't establish the beat so much as it tumbles down into it – there isn't a firm downbeat until the final "yeah" at the end of the fall, and the effect is like jumping on to a moving train.'[70] On that final 'yeah' Ringo bashes on the hi-hat and 'George sneaks in a ratty little guitar lick beneath the vocals, riding out the pleasure that's released to the breaking point. When the first verse begins, it's like a whole new world opening – the music defines ecstasy.'[71] The film is at pains to record that ecstasy, editing together climactic shots of band and audience. The central catalyst to this communal euphoria is the refrain 'yeah, yeah, yeah' – an affirmation so synonymous with the Beatles that it became their alternative name on continental Europe. To this must be added the falsetto 'ooh', to which Paul and George always shook their long hair and, as recorded in *A Hard Day's Night*, consequently raised still further the level of audience hysteria. So well-known was the Beatles' televised performance of this song that Lester to some extent bypasses the group's performance, to add further sight gags – McCartney Senior coming up through the trapdoor, the television director slumped over his console in nervous exhaustion – but mainly to dwell on the audience. Before this final number we see twenty seconds of audience frenzy.

Then, with eight separate cuts from the Beatles to the audience, we see the group for a total of sixty-three seconds, their screaming fans for seventy-six seconds, including a full half-minute immediately preceding the final chorus. As the Beatles sing their last long 'yeah' and the fans cry out for more, we complete our vicarious experience of the final explosion, the song that has given John his wish to blow the Shadows out and, in Tim Riley's words, 'blasts the future of rock wide open'.[72] As the group take their final bow, there bursts into light behind them a large electrical sign. There is no visual play on images here as the sign declares in large illuminated lettering: 'BEATLES'. Lest we forget, the brand name shines out at internal and external audience. The fans can revert to consumers. We can now leave to buy the associated tea towels, shirts, plastic models and, of course, the soundtrack album. *A Hard Day's Night* may not follow the traditional musical in selling marriage, gender fixity or communal stability, but it unmistakably sells the merits of capitalism.

The phenomenon known as 'Beatlemania' was a commercial enterprise whose boundaries went beyond the cinematic into the worlds of music, fashion, even language and a life-enhancing belief. These examples of a 'totalising' culture may have struck the knowing George as 'grotty', but style-guru Simon was right that everyone would want to buy in. And this is the final, overarching duplicitous duality of *A Hard Day's Night*'s harmony of opposites – its concluding *concordia discors*. As the socio-economic context demonstrates, the film, despite its proclaimed – and widely publicised – stylistic innovations and thematic insurrections, could serve only to reinforce the dominant patriarchal ideology and to promote its burgeoning multinational economic interests.

THREE
Reception and Afterlife

YEAH! YEAH! YEAH!

A Hard Day's Night's recuperation into the mainstream is manifested in the royal seal of approval immediately afforded it. After the London première Princess Margaret, accompanied by her husband, Lord Snowdon, asked Paul what he thought of their screen debut. Paul answered: 'I don't think we are very good, ma'am, but we had a very good producer and director.' The Princess said: 'You have nothing to worry about, it was fine.'[1] Pictures of this meeting featured in blanket coverage of the première from the tabloid press, with headlines such as 'A Royal Shake For Ringo' and 'It's a Right Royal Riot of a Film'.[2] Such press treatment confirmed the sense given at the Royal Command Performance in 1963 that the Beatles were somehow 'by royal appointment', acceptable to all classes and all generations.

The film critics of these newspapers were, on the whole, also captivated by the Beatles' celluloid debut. Dick Richards was typical of the punning praise in following his regal alliteration by writing that 'all Britain is buzzing with the jackpot question: "Has the film clicked?" The answer is definitely: "Yeah! Yeah! Yeah!"' Ian Wright in the *Guardian*, clearly no crystal-ball gazer, named it 'a competent piece of work and no weak attempt to cash in on passing popularity'[3] but most others saw the film as other than the expected 'exploitation' quickie. Dilys Powell was pleasantly surprised: 'Instead of the raw excuse for Beatle-song which I had expected, here was a sharply professional piece, directed with great dash by Richard Lester, boldly photographed by Gilbert Taylor, smartly edited by John Jympson – and acted, as well as thrummed and bawled, with the most likeable aplomb by the Sacred Four.'[4] For Michael Thornton of the *Sunday Express* 'Walter Shenson's 85-minute production is not, I am relieved to say, the usual kind of British pop musical in which a series of hit songs are linked loosely by an incredible plot and unspeakable dialogue.' Instead, he judged it as possessing 'all the ingredients of good cinema – wonderful photography, imaginative direction, and excellent character performances'. Thornton was not alone in being particularly impressed with the scriptwriter's contribution: 'In a diamond-bright script full of laconic, incisive wit, Alun Owen captures, better than anyone else to date, the strange, elusive idiom of the Merseybeat.'[5] For Alexander Walker, 'Alun Owen's excellent script is spiky as a running shoe and meant for the same burst of speed.'[6] A rather wishful Nina Hibbin, however, found it 'less successful' due to 'a slightly sinister something about it which punctures the basic purity of the Beatles' image'.[7]

Dick Richards was again one of many to give much of the credit to Richard Lester. 'He has directed with vital speed and inventiveness and has splendidly brought in the atmosphere of mass juvenile hysteria without overdoing it.' Lester's c.v. was extensively cited, John Coleman typical in recalling Lester as 'a Goons man' before noting how 'the finest minutes here recall that heritage'.[8] Alexander Walker was far from unique in his use of adjectives when writing that 'the zaniest bits exploit the wacky, goonish, surreal personalities of the impulsive Beatles'.

Not least in the list of those receiving encomiums were the Beatles themselves, who drew comparisons with past comic quartets. Cecil Wilson of the *Daily Mail* entitled his review 'Merseybeat Marxes' before opening with the assertion that 'the Marx Brothers exploded back on the screen last night'. This was qualified but not quashed in the small print as he labelled the Beatles 'just as crazily inconsequential, just as endearingly insolent, just as infectiously pleased with themselves and – not consistently but here and there – just as funny as the Marxes'.[9] Dilys Powell also, if more hesitantly, broached the comparison, writing: 'I hope it isn't blasphemous to say I was reminded for a second or two of the Marx Brothers.'

The comic emphasis depended on which Beatle was seen as cinematically dominant. For John Coleman the film centred on John Lennon, whose 'weird, sleepily hooded face' is 'somehow allowed to dictate a style for the piece'. His 'anarchic words and deeds' notably the 'Give us a kiss' to the City gent, 'aren't that far off the true Groucho trail'. Looking further back for cultural comparisons, Leonard Mosley fixed the focus very much on Ringo. 'He is the only one of the Beatles who doesn't really like the sound of his own voice. Now I see why. He doesn't need to talk. He is a natural clown in the Chaplin–Harpo Marx class.' More than this, Mosley saw Ringo's 'sad face crowned by the most eloquent nasal organ since Schnozzle Durante and Cyrano de Bergerac'.[10] Penelope Gilliatt agreed that 'Ringo emerges as a born actor. He is like a silent comedian, speechless and chronically underprivileged, a boy who is already ageless.' For her the film highlighted the 'pure comedy' of the Beatles' lives and situation: 'four highly characterised people caught in a series of intensely public dilemmas but always remaining untouched by them, like Keaton, because they cart their private world around everywhere'.[11]

Above all, though, the film succeeded in its aim of personalising its constituent parts. Especially for the older generation of movie critics, the multi-headed hydra from Merseyside was transformed into four highly characterised individuals. For Michael Thornton the film's great surprise was 'the extent to which the four boys emerge as personalities in their own right'. Isabel Quigly was not alone in confessing: 'I could no more have told Ringo from the rest than I could have named Babar in an identity parade of elephants.' Though the metaphor seems too nasally knowing, Quigly insists that initially 'I seemed to be gazing at indistinguishable quadrupeds, trying to disentangle which nose was whose and where eight almost fringe-concealed eyes belonged.' After half an hour, she asserts that the confusion was over for ever.[12] With this individuality came cross-generational acceptance. Felix Barker of the *Evening News* wrote from the perspective of 'many a parent' for whom 'a year's intensive propaganda from the nursery' had given 'a built-in apathy'. Thus writing 'as a man who until this week didn't know Ringo from Paul or George from John (and cared rather less) let me join in the high-pitched, frenzied screaming of teenage enthusiasm'.[13] The words that Barker and many employed were 'off-beat', 'charm' and 'innocence'.

The supporting cast was generally praised, with occasional mentions for Norman Rossington and Victor Spinetti. Most plaudits went to Wilfrid Brambell, who for Alexander Walker 'scuttles through the story like an old fighting crab' and provides 'the professional mainstay of many scenes. It would be far less exuberant a film if the Beatles hadn't got so well-matched an adversary.' Mosley agreed that it was 'an inspiration to cast him in the film. He makes a fine foil for the Beatles.' For Powell he was 'astutely calculating as the centrifugal force'. Only Patrick Gibbs found the character 'tiresome both in the writing and the playing'. But then he also was alone in writing of the Beatles that 'little effort is made to differentiate them or establish independent personalities'.[14]

Few critics made much of the documentary feel of the movie: only

Penelope Gilliatt made mention of the Maysles brothers' work, concluding that 'Dick Lester's film hasn't very much to do with *cinéma-vérité* in its character'. Instead she thought that *A Hard Day's Night* was better described as 'a piece of feature journalism; this is the first film in England that has anything like the urgency and dash of an English popular daily at its best. Like a news feature, it was produced under pressure and the head of steam behind it has produced something expressive and alive.'

This 'tabloid' movie earned itself a maturely reflected review in the most prominent intellectual film journal of the time, *Sight & Sound*. If one excepts *Expresso Bongo* with its respectable literary antecedents and established cast-list, *A Hard Day's Night* was the first British pop musical to be reviewed by the heavyweight journal since *The Tommy Steele Story* some seven years earlier. This demonstrates how the critical establishment were coming to realise that the enormous success of the Beatles required that their film debut should be taken, if not altogether seriously, then at least as a significant and prominent artefact of popular culture. Following pieces on François Truffaut's *La Peau Douce* and Peter Brook's *Lord of the Flies*, Geoffrey Nowell-Smith's review began with the observation that, like the Beatles themselves, or itself, the whole was greater than the sum of its parts. In spite of undistinguished direction, writing and acting, '*eppur si muove*: and yet it works'. Indeed, for Nowell-Smith it works 'on a level at which most British films, particularly the bigger and more pretentious, don't manage to get going at all'. He compares *A Hard Day's Night* with a typical quality British production like Harold Pinter and Jack Clayton's *The Pumpkin Eater* (1964) – 'so carefully thought out, so meticulously scripted, so acted, so heavily "directed", so thoroughly pedantic and ultimately so worked over that it becomes totally self-cancelling'. By contrast the 'skeletal dialogue' of *A Hard Day's Night* together with the 'casual camerawork' and 'the non-acting – none of which would pass muster in a respectable American musical', combine to 'give the effect of an improvisation aimed at projecting a universally appealing image of the amiable happy-go-lucky creatures who are at the centre of it all, precariously poised between Liverpool, Soho and a fairyland of their own invention. The effect is consistently harmless and agreeable, and in all fairness one could hardly ask more than that.' But Nowell-Smith does ask more, and undercuts much of this faintly condescending praise by pointing out 'a lot of British B-Picture badness' which should have been eliminated, and by criticising the final concert scenes which 'whether through cowardice or plain clumsiness have been totally emasculated'. The mediated distancing of group and fans 'produces none of the devastating debunking effect of the candid camera in *Lonely Boy*' (Wolf Koenig and Roman Kroiter's 1962 *cinéma-vérité* short on Paul Anka) with the makers opting for a pretty film at all costs, 'but at a price of honesty and with a wastage of talent which makes one wonder just how far it was all worth while'.[15]

As to its place in the pop musical genre, the review in the equally highbrow *Monthly Film Bulletin* found *A Hard Day's Night* 'streets ahead in imagination compared to other films about pop songs and singers'.[16] It was an evaluation shared with the mainstream magazine critics such as John Coleman who noted how the film engages 'without lowering itself to the sugary depths of a Cliff Richard musical'. Isabel Quigly, recalling the previous week's release of *Wonderful Life*, concluded that 'their whole style, not just of singing, but of behaving ... of taking things quizzically and giving as good as they get, makes Cliff Richard last week seem like a cream-fed domestic cat compared with a litter of perfectly groomed jaguars'.

However, there were several howevers from the critical establishment. David Robinson of *The Times* bemoaned the thinness of plot. Admitting to the group's 'personal qualities quite exceptional to pop groups' he felt that, if cast in a strongly plotted conventional comedy ' – used, in fact as the Will Hay entourage or Formby or Gracie Fields use to be used – I suspect they might have been admirable'. Instead he bemoans their being 'thrown into a shapeless improvisation' where 'the inconsequence and indiscipline and artificial striving for speed are in the end tiring and tedious'.[17] In the United States, the 'zany', 'wacky', 'Goonish' humour and, in particular, the decision to remain true to the Liverpool accent were features not appreciated by all: John Seelye of *Film Quarterly* remarked that 'some sequences of this film need subtitles'.[18] And the *Time* film critic noted that 'sometimes the humor seems forced, the North Country slang impenetrable' before advocating instead the Maysles brothers' recent documentary for its 'more exciting and at the same time more perceptive view of a Beatle's insular existence'.[19]

Such criticisms were still very much in the minority. In the ultimate critical soundbite Andrew Sarris of the American magazine *Village Voice* described the film as 'the "Citizen Kane" of jukebox musicals'.[20] The analogy to an American masterpiece is doubly apposite, since not only does it suggest a qualitative evaluation, but also *A Hard Day's Night* constituted the first ever British pop musical to break into the American market. Cliff Richard had secured success almost everywhere else in the world, but the American continent remained stubbornly resistant to his and all other British charms. Prior to their February tour of the United States, the Beatles had also been worried about their chances. Hunter Davies notes that 'George said he'd seen Cliff's film *Summer Holiday* reduced to the second feature in a drive-in in St Louis'.[21] By the time the film was completed, though, even they knew that such fears were groundless. Nowhere resisted 'Beatlemania'.

TO GET YOU MONEY. TO BUY YOU THINGS

Box-office profits for *A Hard Day's Night* were phenomenal. Made for under £200,000 ($350,000), the film brought in $5,800,000 in US rentals in six weeks, and around $14 million world gross. As well as the album and single tie-ins, the film was shrewdly released just prior to the Beatles' second US tour in August. It must be stressed, though, that while *A Hard Day's Night* is a British film in that it employed British cast and crew, its financing came from and therefore its profits went to, United Artists, an American company. In this, it set the trend for the rest of the 1960s: that of Hollywood financing the British look that was doing so well at the box-office. As with the James Bond films, *Alfie, Georgy Girl* and others, *A Hard Day's Night* is quintessentially British in its ideology, but its economics are entirely American.

For the only time in the history of the British pop musical, the film also received two Academy Award nominations, Alun Owen for original script and George Martin for soundtrack. *A Hard Day's Night* was the second most profitable film of 1964 in Britain, just behind the James Bond film *Goldfinger*. Third came *Zulu* (again edited by Jympson), then Norman Wisdom's *A Stitch in Time*, and fifth Cliff's *Wonderful Life*: thus, uniquely, the five biggest money-makers for 1964 were all, nominally, British films. Nevertheless, the Beatles were only the eighth most popular film stars of the year, some way behind Cliff Richard (second) and Elvis Presley, who that year released his tenth film, *Kissing Cousins*, and came in fourth, Sean Connery heading this particular Top 10.

No one, though, could prevent the Beatles' total domination of the music charts. 'Can't Buy Me Love' had been released at the end of March, prior to the film's completion. The song entered the British charts at number one, spent four weeks at the top spot and a total of fourteen weeks in the charts. It was the third Beatles single in a row to sell over a million copies in the UK. In the United States 'Can't Buy Me Love' set a new record for advance sales, with orders for 2,100,000 copies. The song spent five weeks at number 1, and ten weeks in the Hot 100. The B-side, 'You Can't Do That', also made the Top 50, making it double-A-sided hit. It was also a major hit around the world.

The title-track from the Beatles' first film was issued in Britain on 10 July 1964, and in America three days later. 'A Hard Day's Night' entered the British charts straight at number 1 and remained there for four weeks in Britain and for two weeks in America, spending a total of thirteen weeks in the charts on both sides of the Atlantic. In America the B-side also charted: 'I Should Have Known Better' reached number 53 during four weeks in the *Billboard* charts. (The British B-side was 'Things We Said Today'.) Actually, the single was the Beatles' first since 'From Me to You' not to sell a million in Britain, though it did reach that figure in America and global sales were several million. 'A Hard Day's Night' was the Beatles' biggest international hit up to that time, hitting the number 1 spot in Britain, the USA, Ireland, Australia, South Africa, Finland, Sweden, Norway, Germany, the Netherlands, Spain, Malaysia, Singapore and Hong Kong. Significantly, it also topped the charts in Argentina, and reached the Top 5 in Brazil, Peru and Uruguay. Having been the first British artists to conquer North America, the Beatles were helped by this film to conquer South America as well. To cap its success, the song won a Grammy Award for Best Vocal Group Performance of 1964. (Also, much to the group's satisfaction, their Goon hero Peter Sellers recorded a comic take on the song, which reached number 15 in the British charts the following year.)

The initial *raison d'être* for the film, its soundtrack album, was issued in America by United Artists on 26 June 1964, two weeks before Parlophone issued an album of the same name in Britain. These are in fact different products: the American record is the film soundtrack, including four instrumental tracks by the George Martin Orchestra – Martin had a personal recording contract with United Artists for America – whereas the British release consists of the group's recordings of songs featured in the film, plus other new material. Both albums were recorded at EMI's Abbey Road studios and produced by George Martin from the same takes, though here again, the mixes were sometimes different as, for instance, on the title-track.

Though different in content, the two albums achieved the same phenomenal success. In Britain, *A Hard Day's Night*, the Beatles' third 'home' album, stayed at number 1 in the album charts for twenty-one weeks (to be replaced by *Beatles for Sale*), and spent a total of thirty-eight weeks in the charts. The record sold close to 700,000 copies in Britain in its first year of release, with European sales well over a million. In America the soundtrack album had an advance order of a million and soon doubled that figure in sales. It went to number 1 for fourteen weeks, keeping the 'rival' Capitol album *Something New* (which contained five of the songs also on the soundtrack album) blocked at number 2 for nine weeks. In total, the album spent fifty-one weeks on the American charts. (*Something New* spent forty-one weeks in the charts, with eventual sales topping the million mark.) Adding all these albums together, global sales of the soundtrack to *A Hard Day's Night* can be totalled at around 4 million. None of the Beatles' compositions was nominated for an Academy Award, however: in 1964 that honour went to 'Chim-Chim-Cheree' from *Mary Poppins*.

Sheet music sales were also prolific, while the narrative and imagery of the film would fuel numerous lucrative ancillary products such as a novelisation by John Burke (published by Pan Books and including 'eight pages of illustration in photogravure'), an official United Artists' pictorial souvenir book (promising 'candid cameras behind the scenes') and a set of fifty-five black-and-white sepia tone trading cards, franchised to Topp's Chewing Gum Co.

A Hard Day's Night has remained in near-constant circulation. After taking the British pop musical to a whole new level of exposure and economic success, the film was sold to television (NBC paid £1.5 million for US rights) and began small screen-showings from July 1968. In the UK it became a staple fixture of Christmas broadcasting through the early 1970s and brought a whole new generation of fans to the Beatles. When the copyright reverted to Walter Shenson in 1979, he prepared it for rerelease in the USA with a Dolby stereo soundtrack in 1981. He also added a prefix to the film, a series of stills, joined with graphic effects as a background to 'I'll Cry Instead', the number that Lester rejected for the frolic in the fields. Whatever its archival interest, by any aesthetic criteria this was a crass addition, dissipating the effect of the the movie's revelatory opening chord and chase. The film was released on video in America and the United Kingdom in 1984 and at various times thereafter, mostly with Shenson's added opening. The hour-long video entitled *The Making of A Hard Day's Night*, narrated by audience member Phil Collins, was released in early

1996. A remastered two-disc DVD issue came to the United States in 2001, to Great Britain and Europe in 2002, and featured interviews with cast and crew but nothing, alas, from the remaining members of the group. Nor did Paul's deleted scene materialise, apparently destroyed by Twickenham Studio's library in line with its policy of removing all unused footage five years after the completion of a film. Nevertheless the release generated considerable press and magazine coverage, bringing yet more new fans to 'a treasured piece of rock history that remains influential to this day'.[22]

LOOMING LARGE IN THEIR LEGEND

What exactly is that influence? The group themselves followed *A Hard Day's Night* with another world tour, another album (*Beatles for Sale*), a UK tour, a twenty-night run in their Christmas Show, and then allowed themselves a short break before recording the soundtrack and filming their second United Artists venture, eventually titled *Help!* (1965). Richard Lester again directed, but had to do so without Gilbert Taylor, dismayed at what he had seen from behind the camera. It was also decided to dispense with the services of the two Oscar nominees, Owen and Martin. The resultant picture, a colour-supplement Bond spoof, was again a Royal Première and earned as much as its predecessor, but never earned the popular or critical affection afforded *A Hard Day's Night*. More conventionally plotted, and therefore more entrusted to professional actors such as Leo McKern, the film featured the Beatles as, in John's phrase, extras in their own movie.[23] Now caricatured at two removes – scriptwriter Charles Wood tried to learn the group dynamic by watching *A Hard Day's Night* – the group were also distanced by their recent discovery of pot, and the film replicated as much as spoofed the sexist and imperialist codes of Bond and the British Empire. The Beatles, disillusioned, drugged up and distracted by their growing musical experimentations, would only once return to fictional film production, and then briefly in Paul's television movie, *Magical Mystery Tour* (1967).

A Hard Day's Night was more evidently influential on the first film venture for London's answer to the Fab Four, the Dave Clark Five. John Boorman's *Catch Us If You Can* (1965) was again monochrome, art-inspired, but picked up on the 'Can't Buy Me Love' sequence and dispensed entirely with diegetic performance. Boorman's debut, like the Beatles', investigated how a group's music, while remaining the motor of their success, was losing its primary function as their image assumed fuller importance in defining their status as cultural icons. An awareness of and uneasiness with this presentational aspect is a feature of the 'mature' pop musical: *A Hard Day's Night* concerns the Fab Four's fan-filled journey south to a televised variety concert, while *Catch Us If You Can* provides a journey south-west to escape the ubiquitous presence of and presentation through the television cameras. With its quick-fire portrayal of the semiotics of show business, *Catch Us If You Can* was, for Andy Medhurst, the moment that the pop film became the Pop Film.[24] It also signalled the sub-genre's (paradigm) shift to the marginal status that it would subsequently occupy. The sacrificing of conventional narrative also meant the sacrificing of commercial and critical acceptance – as the Beatles found to their cost with the bemused and hostile response that greeted Paul's psychedelic and surreal coach tour. Yet after this radical mid-1960s realignment, there could be no return to the more accessible narrative naïvetés of exploitation quickies like *The Tommy Steele Story* or even ersatz Hollywood offerings like *Summer Holiday* if one hoped for any semblance of credibility. Medhurst cites the misguided, mistimed efforts of Freddie and the Dreamers and John Leyton in *Every Day's a Holiday* (1965) which, though retitled *Seaside Swingers* for the United States, ends with an even more depressing seaside spectacle than Boorman's beach-side break-up. In truth, as Medhurst notes, 'The British pop film, in all its endearing awkwardness, was pretty much dead.'[25]

After the arty Pop Art knowingness kick-started by *A Hard Day's Night* and completed by *Catch Us If You Can*, the only truly cinematic option for rock stars keen to 'branch out' into new artistic territory, and for directors willing to take a chance on unproven acting talent, led inexorably into the final, decadent phase of the British pop musical, a shrinking maze of self-referentiality and psycho-political pretension, an art-house, gestural cinema that, via Peter Watkins's *Privilege* (1967) and Godard's *One Plus One*, would finally implode in the Borgesian gunshot of Donald Cammell and Nicolas Roeg's *Performance* (1970).

From a broader perspective, the financial returns garnered by the Beatles' debut helped to sustain American investment in British cinema throughout the 1960s, a commitment that peaked in 1968 when 88 per cent of British productions enjoyed US funding. This cinematic British invasion was also culturally significant since, as Robert Murphy noted, 'the impact of the Bond movies, *Tom Jones* and *A Hard Day's Night* on the US market changed attitudes towards Britain, fostering a belief that London, rather than Paris or Rome or Hollywood, was the place in the world to make a film'.[26] That opening chase down Boston Place led straight into the wider media construct known as 'Swinging London'.

Though this transatlantic investment imploded at the end of the 1960s, the Beatles' film remains, through association, an entrée to US markets. This was evidenced by the success in 1996 of *Trainspotting* (another BFI 100 entry), consistently likened in the American press to *A Hard Day's Night* for its stylish irreverence, rejection of narrative realism and even its depiction of upward mobility. The reviewer of *New York* noted how Renton and Co. 'jump about Edinburgh chasing down streets like the Beatles in *A Hard Day's Night*, romping in and out of bars or just sitting around making preposterous jokes',[27] while Richard Corliss opined that Danny Boyle's film could 'achieve the cult-hit success of a certain 1964 movie, which was also about four British lads with heavy Northern accents and anti-Establishment cheek and which also began with the boys eluding their pursuers'.[28]

Such crossovers remain the exception, however, and one must look instead to television to discover the enduring influence of the Beatles' first feature film. This is most blatantly evident in the television series *The Monkees* (1966–68), made by Columbia's television division, Screen Gems. Selected from a well-publicised advert in *Variety* magazine (9 September 1965) by young TV producers Bob Rafelson and Bert Schneider, the mop-topped pre-fab four were obviously – and unashamedly – an ersatz Beatles. Michael Nesmith was the deadpan John, Davy Jones the good-looking (and English) Paul, Peter Tork the laconic George, and Micky Dolenz the madcap Ringo. Each kept his real first name and shared a house *Help!*-style, while their group identity even deliberately misspells their animal-name. Each of the fifty-six episodes featured two song sequences, not always diegetically presented. Mark Lewisohn categorised the series thus: 'Mimicking Richard Lester's directorial style of jump cuts, slow- and fast-motion film and odd camera angles prevalent in *A Hard Day's Night* and *Help!*, Rafelson and Schneider created a fast-paced, frenetic TV show combining slapstick, engaging personalities and pop music in roughly equal quantities.'[29] The pop music had its own life, of course, feeding into numerous highly successful spin-off albums. Before *A Hard Day's Night* could find its own second home on television, the Monkees filled the vacant market gap for teenage adulation.

While America's home-grown answer also imploded into overknowing irony and psychedelia, alienating their fan base in their own movie debut *Head* (1968), the Beatles enjoyed/endured a lengthier reincarnation, this time in cartoon form. In November 1964, Brian Epstein signed a contract allowing Al Brodax's US-based King Features company to make fifty-two half-hour shows, using two Beatles songs in each. The show premièred on ABC television on 25 September 1965 (episode one was entitled and featured 'A Hard Day's Night'), immediately broke all US television ratings, and lasted as long as the group itself, closing in September 1969. This proved to be a constant bone of contention within the group. The problem was that – like so many of Brian Epstein's early incompetent negotiations when overwhelmed in the first wave of Beatlemania – it provided a distinctly bum deal for the group, who received little financial return and zero creative imput. Second, throughout the late 1960s the group had to put up with impersonated anachronisms as the still lovably mop-topped caricatures 'ad-libbed' in *A Hard Day's Night* style while delivering the psychedelic sounds of 'Strawberry Fields' and 'All You Need is Love'. With the exception of George and his new Eastern interests, this 1964 characterisation – plus Ringo as plot motor – would again inform King Features' full-length animation *Yellow Submarine* (1968), a project the Beatles initially disowned, but came to endorse with a hastily filmed coda, largely in the hope that this would complete their three-film deal with United Artists. It did not, hence the studio documentary *Let It Be*.

A Hard Day's Night continues to resonate in the television cartoon genre. Constituting the ultimate postmodern *palmares*, the film is heavily referenced in an episode of *The Simpsons*. The end credits to 'The Old Man and the "C" Student'[30] ape the red, four-frame structure of the film's original US soundtrack album; when Grandpa Simpson plus the other old-age inmates escape from their Retirement Castle to race around Springfield, the sequence effects a neat generational reverse by mirroring the playing field antics of the Beatles – this time the senior delinquents' 'Can't Buy Me Love' accompaniment is sung by NRBQ.

In retrospect, the greatest influence of *A Hard Day's Night* emanates from that single song and its cinematic illustration, filmed at Gatwick and Isleworth over three days early in 1964. Its effect on the visual language of popular music, breaking the song free from imitative performance in a diegetic mode, leads, via the Alps-set 'Ticket to Ride' sequence in *Help!*, directly into the fab format of the group's mid-1960s internationally distributed promos shot by Joe McGrath, Michael Lindsay-Hogg and Peter Goldmann. The latter's revisiting of the group messing about in fields on 'Strawberry Fields Forever' had considerable impact on the form and function of the nascent pop video, which eventually led to the pilot programme *Pop Clips* and the launching on 1 August 1981 of MTV and the marketing of popular music as we know it today. Amid the lengthy genealogy, it is a significant symmetry that MTV was set up by former Monkee, and hence Lester epigone, Mike Nesmith. (It constitutes the final doubleness of *A Hard Day's Night* that the commercial *raison d'être* for the pop musical film was rendered obsolete by its commercial apogee.) On the DVD commentary accompanying the film, Lester tells of being sent a vellum scroll citing him as 'the father of MTV'. With a typical mocking of generational intolerance, his reply was to insist on a blood test.

Lester's bloodline is clear in the video for Beatles wannabes Oasis's 'Wonderwall' (1995), which includes multiple black-and-white images of the Gallagher brothers. He should also look to paternity suits for recent feature film ventures back into the world of pop music culture. The poster to *High Fidelity* (2000), telling the story of pop music obsessive Rob Gordon, again copies the iconographic style of Robert Freeman's Beatles original, while the opening credits of *Austin Powers: International Man of Mystery* (1997) immediately create a 1960s setting by having the eponymous celebrity spy run from his screaming fans down a narrow car-lined pavement, then sport a false beard and hide behind a magazine and in a telephone box. Above all, *Spiceworld: The Movie* (1997), while employing Cliff's red double-decker bus from *Summer Holiday*, structures itself as a new-millennium Lesteroid, with the 'wacky' Spice Girls facing madcap adventures and finding themselves up against the clock in their attempt to make their important closing concert. That Britain's first major pop musical in over thirty years should present itself so openly as a homage to the Beatles' own film debut demonstrates how, in spite of new technical developments in the video and digital age, the textual premise of Lester's 1960s movie, the illustrative aesthetic of non-performance mode, has passed on from generation to generation. *A Hard Day's Night* continues to constitute the very lifeblood of filmed popular music, and fully justifies its place in the BFI's Top 100.

Notes

1. CONTEXT

1. Marwick, *The Sixties*, p. 7.
2. Marwick, *British Society since 1945*, p. 13.
3. Richards and Aldgate, *Best of British: Cinema and Society 1930–1970*, p. 111.
4. Bicat, 'Fifties Children: Sixties People', in Bogdanor and Skidelsky (eds), *The Age of Affluence 1951–1964*, p. 324.
5. Ibid.
6. Hebdige, *Hiding in the Light: On Images and Things*, p. 19.
7. Hill, *Sex, Class and Realism: British Cinema 1956–1963*, pp. 117–18.
8. Anonymous, *The Times*, 31 October 1960.
9. Gillett, *The Sound of the City*, p. 256.
10. Cohn, *Awopbopaloobop Alopbamboom: Pop from the Beginning*, p. 75.
11. Bradley, *Understanding Rock'n'Roll: Popular Music in Britain 1955–64*, p. 71.
12. Gillett, *The Sound of the City*, p. 257.
13. Turner, *Cliff Richard: The Biography*, p. 143.
14. Melly, *Revolt into Style*, p. 70.
15. Murphy, *Sixties British Cinema*, p. 135.
16. Richard Dyer, *The Movie*, No. 75, p. 1484
17. Hayward, *Key Concepts in Cinema Studies*, p. 241.
18. John Coleman, *New Statesman*, 3 July 1964.
19. Melly, *Revolt into Style*, p. 167.
20. Carr, *Beatles at the Movies*, p. 23.
21. Sinyard, *The Films of Richard Lester*, p. 5.
22. Walker, *Hollywood England*, p. 222.
23. Ibid.
24. Ibid.
25. Sinyard, *The Films of Richard Lester*, p. 7.
26. Philip French, *Movie*, No. 14, Autumn 1965.
27. Walker, *Hollywood England*, p. 222.

28. Dilys Powell, *Sunday Times*, 1 April 1962.
29. Isabel Quigly, *The Spectator*, 6 April 1962.
30. David Robinson, *The Times*, 29 March 1962.
31. *You Can't Do That: The Making of A Hard Day's Night* – video release.
32. Carr, *Beatles at the Movies*, p. 30.
33. Ibid.
34. Robin Bean, 'Keeping up with the Beatles', *Films and Filming*, February 1964, p. 12.
35. Miles, *Paul McCartney: Many Years From Now*, p. 158.
36. Richard Lester, interviewed in Soderbergh, *Getting Away With It*, p. 29.
37. George Melly, *Guardian*, 8 December 1994.
38. Carr, *Beatles at the Movies*, p. 33.
39. Walker, *Hollywood England*, pp. 234–5.
40. Harry, *The Ultimate Beatles Encyclopedia*, p. 505.
41. Ibid., p. 506.
42. Evans, *The Art of the Beatles*, p. 26.
43. Quoted in Carr, *Beatles at the Movies*, p. 44.
44. Ibid.
45. Balio, *United Artists: The Company Built by Stars*, p. 250.
46. Walker, *Hollywood England*, p. 239.
47. Harry, *The Ultimate Beatles Encyclopedia*, p. 286.
48. *Mojo*, No. 108, November 2002, p. 74.
49. Miles, *Paul McCartney: Many Years from Now*, p. 164.
50. Lennon, *In His Own Write*, p. 29.
51. Coleman, *Lennon: The Definitive Biography*, p. 360.
52. Walker, *Hollywood England*, p. 240.
53. *Hollywood UK*, BBC broadcast, September 1993.
54. Walker, *Hollywood England*, p. 229–30.
55. Carr, *Beatles at the Movies*, p. 47.

2. ANALYSIS

1. MacDonald, *Revolution in the Head*, p. 102.
2. Coleman, *Lennon: The Definitive Biography*, p. 316.
3. Ann Scott-Jones, *Daily Mail*, 16 July 1964.
4. Quoted in di Franco, *The Beatles in Richard Lester's A Hard Day's Night*, p. 5.
5. Buskin, *Beatle Crazy! Memories and Memorabilia*, pp. 10–11.

NOTES

6. Frith, 'Rock and the Politics of Memory', in Sayres et al. (eds), *The Sixties without Apology*, p. 60.
7. Gillett, *The Sound of the City*, p. 312.
8. Melly, *Revolt into Style*, p. 73.
9. Quoted in Walker, *Hollywood England*, p. 237.
10. Richard Lester quoted in di Franco, *The Beatles in Richard Lester's A Hard Day's Night*, p. 5.
11. Gelmis (ed.), *The Film Director as Superstar*, p. 316.
12. Howard Jacobson, 'Resignation Letters', *Times Literary Supplement*, 21 January 2000, p. 20.
13. Harker, *One for the Money: The Politics of Popular Song*, p. 84.
14. Walker, *Hollywood England*, p. 239.
15. Kureishi and Savage (eds), *The Faber Book of Pop*, p. xix.
16. Brown and Gaines, *The Love You Make*, pp. 116–17.
17. Carr, *Beatles at the Movies*, p. 16.
18. Hayward, *Key Concepts in Cinema Studies*, p. 155.
19. Braun, *"Love me Do!"*, p. 32.
20. Coleman, *Lennon: The Definitive Biography*, pp. 315–18.
21. Bourne, *Brief Encounters: Lesbians and Gays in British Cinema 1930–1971*, p. 184.
22. Ibid.
23. Ibid.
24. Ibid.
25. ibid., p. 185.
26. *The Beatles Anthology*, shown on ITV, December 1995.
27. Neaverson, *The Beatles Movies*, p. 21.
28. Brown and Gaines, *The Love You Make*, p. 118.
29. Paul Johnson, *New Statesman*, 28 February 1964, reprinted in Kureishi and Savage (eds), *The Faber Book of Pop*, p. 197.
30. Angela McRobbie and Jenny Garber, 'Girls and Subcultures: an Exploration', in Clarke et al. (eds), *Resistance Through Rituals*, p. 221.
31. Lewis, *The Road to Romance and Ruin*, p. 88.
32. Catterall and Wells, *Your Face Here: British Cult Movies Since the Sixties*, p. 14.
33. Eric Rhode, *Sight & Sound*, Vol. 30, No. 1, Winter 1960/61, p. 34; Penelope Gilliatt, *Observer*, 12 July 1964.
34. Gillett, *The Sound of the City*, p. 313.
35. Whiteley, *Pop Design: Modernism to Mod*, p. 102.
36. Quoted in the video *You Can't Do That: The Making of A Hard Day's Night*.

37. Brown and Gaines, *The Love You Make*, p. 116.
38. Melly, *Revolt into Style*, p. 69.
39. Meltzer, *The Aesthetics of Rock*, pp. 13–14.
40. Walker, *Hollywood England*, p. 240.
41. Shanes, *Warhol: The Masterworks*, p. 100.
42. Honnof, *Andy Warhol*, p. 68.
43. Walter Spies, quoted in ibid.
44. Lewis, *The Road to Romance and Ruin*, p. 89.
45. Neaverson, *The Beatles Movies*, p. 17.
46. Quoted in *The Beatles Anthology*, p. 128.
47. Quoted in *Hollywood UK*, BBC broadcast, September 1993.
48. Braun, *"Love Me Do!"*, p. 74.
49. Feuer, *The Hollywood Musical*, p. 107.
50. Quoted in *The Beatles Anthology*, p. 129.
51. Mundy, *Popular Music on Screen*, pp. 172–3.
52. Melly, *Revolt into Style*, p. 75.
53. Mellers, *Twilight of the Gods: The Beatles in Retrospect*, p. 34.
54. Ibid., p. 39.
55. Ibid., p. 43.
56. Ibid., p. 45.
57. MacDonald, *Revolution in the Head*, p. 97.
58. Ibid., p. 99.
59. Quoted in *You Can't Do That: The Making of A Hard Day's Night*.
60. Sinyard, *The Films of Richard Lester*, p. 25.
61. Evans, *The Art of the Beatles*, p. 131.
62. Wheen, *The Sixties*, p. 23.
63. Trevor Philpott, *Picture Post*, 25 February 1957.
64. Ehrenreich et al., 'Beatlemania: Girls Just Want to Have Fun', in Lewis (ed.), *The Adoring Audience: Fan Culture and Popular Media*, p. 97.
65. Mundy, *Popular Music on Screen*, p. 172.
66. di Franco, *The Beatles in Richard Lester's A Hard Day's Night*, p. 31.
67. Ehrenreich et al. in Lewis (ed.), *The Adoring Audience: Fan Culture and Popular Media*, p. 55.
68. L. Grossberg, 'Is There a Fan in the House? The Affective Sensibility of Fandom', in Lewis (ed.), *The Adoring Audience: Fan Culture and Popular Media*, p. 55.
69. Ibid., p. 56.
70. Riley, *Tell Me Why*, p. 67.

NOTES

71. Ibid.
72. Ibid., p. 66.

3. RECEPTION AND AFTERLIFE

1. Carr, *Beatles at the Movies*, p. 48.
2. Dick Richards, *Daily Mirror*, 8 July 1964.
3. Ian Wright, *Guardian*, 7 July 1964.
4. Dilys Powell, *Sunday Times*, 12 July 1964.
5. Michael Thornton, *Sunday Express*, 13 July 1964.
6. Alexander Walker, *Evening Standard*, 6 July 1964.
7. Nina Hibbin, *Daily Worker*, 7 July 1964.
8. John Coleman, *New Statesman*, 10 July 1964.
9. Cecil Wilson, *Daily Mail*, 7 July, 1964.
10. Leonard Mosley, *Daily Express*, 7 July 1964.
11. Penelope Gilliatt, *Observer*, 12 July, 1964.
12. Isabel Quigly, *The Spectator*, 10 July 1964.
13. Felix Barker, *Evening News*, 9 July 1964.
14. Patrick Gibbs, *Daily Telegraph*, 7 July 1964.
15. Geoffrey Nowell-Smith, *Sight & Sound*, Vol. 33, No. 4, Autumn 1964, pp. 196–7.
16. *Monthly Film Bulletin*, August 1964.
17. David Robinson, *The Times*, 10 July 1964.
18. John Seelye, *Film Quarterly*, Autumn 1964, p. 54.
19. Anonymous, *Time*, 4 August 1964.
20. Andrew Sarris, *Village Voice*, 27 August 1964.
21. Davies, *The Beatles*, p. 212.
22. Covernotes to *The Beatles' "A Hard Day's Night" DVD 2 Disc Collector's Edition*, Miramax, 2002.
23. Coleman, *Lennon: The Definitive Biography*, p. 369.
24. Andy Medhurst, 'It Sort of Happened Here', in Romney and Wootton (eds), *Celluloid Jukebox*, p. 68.
25. Ibid., pp. 68–9.
26. Murphy, *Sixties British Cinema*, p. 114.
27. Anonymous, *New York*, 12 August 1996.
28. Richard Corliss, *Time*, 15 July 1996.
29. Lewisohn, *Radio Times Guide to TV Comedy*, p. 445.
30. Episode AABF16, original airdate: 25 April 1999.

Sources

NEWSPAPERS AND PERIODICALS

Chapter notes indicate the newspapers and periodicals used for film reviews. These were mostly taken from the British Film Institute's microfiche film collection. Quotations come from reviews and articles in the following British newspapers and periodicals: *Daily Express*, *Daily Mail*, *Daily Mirror*, *Daily Telegraph*, *Daily Worker*, *Evening News*, *Evening Standard*, *Guardian*, *New Statesman*, *Observer*, *Picture Post*, *Spectator*, *Sunday Express*, *Sunday Times*, and *The Times*.

BOOKS

Aldgate, Anthony, James Chapman and Arthur Marwick (eds), *Windows on the Sixties* (London: I.B. Tauris, 2000).

Balio, Tino, *United Artists: The Company Built by the Stars* (Wisconsin: University of Wisconsin, 1987).

Bogdanor, Vernon and Robert Skidelsky (eds), *The Age of Affluence 1951–1964* (London: Macmillan, 1970).

Bourne, Stephen, *Brief Encounters: Lesbians and Gays in British Cinema 1930–1971* (London: Cassell, 1996).

Bradley, Dick, *Understanding Rock'n'Roll: Popular Music in Britain 1955–64* (Milton Keynes: Open University Press, 1992).

Braun, Michael, *"Love Me Do!"* (Harmondsworth: Penguin, 1964).

Brown, Peter and Steven Gaines, *The Love You Make* (London: Pan, 1984).

Buskin, Richard, *Beatle Crazy! Memories and Memorabilia* (London: Salamander, 1994).

Carr, Roy, *Beatles at the Movies: Scenes From a Career* (London: UFO Music, 1996).

Catterall, Ali and Simon Wells, *Your Face Here: British Cult Movies Since the Sixties* (London: Fourth Estate, 2001).

Clarke, John, Stuart Hall, Tony Jefferson and Brian Roberts, *Resistance Through Rituals* (London: Hutchinson, 1976).

Cohn, Nik, *Awopbopaloobop Alopbamboom: Pop from the Beginning* (London: Weidenfeld and Nicolson, 1969).

Coleman, Ray, *Lennon: The Definitive Biography* (London: Pan, 1995).

Davies, Hunter, *The Beatles* (London: Heinemann, 1968).

di Franco, J. Philip, *The Beatles in Richard Lester's A Hard Day's Night – a Complete Pictorial Record of the Movie* (Harmondsworth: Penguin, 1977).

Evans, Mike, *The Art of the Beatles* (London: Anthony Blond, 1984).

Feuer, Jane, *The Hollywood Musical* (London: Macmillan, 1982).

Gelmis, Joseph (ed.), *The Film Director as Superstar* (London: Secker and Warburg, 1971).

Gillett, Charlie, *The Sound of the City* (London: Sphere, 1971).

Harker, Dave, *One for the Money: The Politics of Popular Song* (London: Hutchinson, 1980).

Harry, Bill, *The Ultimate Beatles Encyclopedia* (London: Virgin, 1992).

Hayward, Susan, *Key Concepts in Cinema Studies* (London: Routledge, 1996).

Hebdige, Dick, *Hiding in the Light: On Images and Things* (London: Routledge, 1989).

Hill, John, *Sex, Class and Realism: British Cinema 1956–1963* (London: British Film Institute, 1986).

Honnof, Klaus, *Andy Warhol* (Berlin: Taschen, 1990).

Kureishi, Hanif and Jon Savage, *The Faber Book of Pop* (London: Faber, 1995).

Lennon, John, *In His Own Write* (London: Cape, 1964).

Lewis, Jon, *The Road to Romance and Ruin* (London: Routledge, 1992).

Lewis, L.A. (ed.), *The Adoring Audience: Fan Culture and Popular Media* (London: Routledge, 1992).

Lewisohn, Mark, *Radio Times Guide to TV Comedy* (London: BBC, 1998).

MacDonald, Ian, *Revolution in the Head* (London: Fourth Estate, 1994).

Marwick, Arthur, *British Society Since 1945*, 3rd edn (London: Penguin, 1996).

— *The Sixties: Cultural Revolution in Britain, France, Italy and the United States c. 1958–1974* (Oxford: Oxford University Press, 1998).

Mellers, Wilfrid, *Twilight of the Gods: The Beatles in Retrospect* (London: Faber, 1973).

Melly, George, *Revolt into Style* (Harmondsworth: Penguin, 1972).

Meltzer, Richard, *The Aesthetics of Rock* (New York: Da Capo, 1987).

Miles, Barry, *Paul McCartney: Many Years from Now* (London: Secker and Warburg, 1997).

Mundy, John, *Popular Music on Screen: From Hollywood Musical to Musical Video* (Manchester: Manchester University Press, 1999).

Murphy, Robert, *Sixties British Cinema* (London: British Film Institute, 1992).

Neaverson, Bob, *The Beatles Movies* (London: Cassell, 1997).

Richards, Jeffrey and Anthony Aldgate, *Best of British: Cinema and Society 1930–1970* (Oxford: Basil Blackwell, 1983).

Riley, Tim, *Tell Me Why* (London: Bodley Head, 1988).

Romney, Jonathan and Andrew Wootton (eds), *Celluloid Jukebox: Popular Music and the Movies since the '50s* (London: British Film Institute, 1995).

Sayres, Sonya, Anders Stephenson, Stanley Aronowitz and Frederic Jameson (eds), *The Sixties without Apology*, (Minneapolis: University of Minneapolis Press, 1984).

Shanes, Eric, *Warhol: The Masterworks* (London: Studio Editions, 1991).

Sinyard, Neil, *The Films of Richard Lester* (Beckenham: Croom Hill, 1985).

Soderbergh, Steven, *Getting Away with It* (London: Faber, 1999).

Turner, Steve, *Cliff Richard: The Biography* (Oxford: Lion Publishing, 1993).

Walker, Alexander, *Hollywood England* (London: Harrap, 1986).

Wheen, Francis, *The Sixties* (London: Century/Channel 4, 1982).

Whiteley, Nigel, *Pop Design: Modernism to Mod*, (London: Design Council, 1987).